IDIOTS TO MONSTERS

THE ESSENTIAL GUIDE TO SURVIVING COMMON THREATS AND VIOLENT ENCOUNTERS

DAVID A. KERR   LUKE STROCKIS

HARRISON LEBOWITZ

DEFENSE KINETICS PUBLISHING

Defense Kinetics Publishing

1024 Bayside Drive #335

Newport Beach, CA 92660

info@defensekinetics.com

www.defensekinetics.com

(888) 803-3566

ISBN: 978-1-7338034-0-3

ISBN: 978-1-7338034-1-0 (eBook)

Edited and Formatted by: Kristen Forbes (deviancepress.com)

Cover Design by: Design Studio Nuovo

Photos courtesy of Luke Strockis, unless otherwise noted.

10 9 8 7 6 5 4 3 2

Title: *Idiots to Monsters: The Essential Guide to Surviving Common Threats and Violent Encounters* / David A. Kerr with Luke Strockis and Harrison Lebowitz.

Description: Newport Beach, CA USA: Defense Kinetics Publishing, [2019] | Includes bibliographical references and index.

Subjects: LCSH: Self-defense—Handbooks, manuals, etc. | Self-defense—Psychological aspects | Violence—Psychological aspects. | Violence—Prevention—Handbooks, manuals, etc., | Crime prevention—Handbooks, manuals, etc., | Martial arts—Handbooks, manuals, etc., | Martial Arts—Psychological aspects. | Fighting (Psychology) | Criminal psychology. | BISAC: SPORTS & RECREATION / Martial Arts & Self-Defense. | SOCIAL SCIENCE / Criminology. | SOCIAL SCIENCE / Violence in Society. SOCIAL SCIENCE / Criminology. | SOCIAL SCIENCE / Violence in Society.

manner whatsoever for any injury which may occur through reading or following the instructions in this guide book.

The activities, physical or otherwise, described in this manual may be too strenuous or dangerous for some people, and the reader(s) should consult a physician before engaging in them.

Warning: While self-defense is legal, fighting is illegal. Readers are encouraged to be aware of all appropriate local and national laws relating to self-defense, reasonable force, and the use of weaponry, and to act in accordance with all applicable laws. Be aware and understand that while legal definitions and interpretations are generally uniform, there are significant and very important differences from state to state and even city to city. To avoid criminal charges, you must understand these differences. Neither the authors nor publisher assume any responsibility for the use or misuse of information contained in this book.

Nothing in this document constitutes a legal opinion, nor should any of its contents be treated as such. While the authors believe everything herein is accurate, any questions regarding specific self-defense situations, legal liability, and/or interpretation of federal, state, or local laws should always be addressed by an attorney at law.

When it comes to martial arts, self-defense, self-protection, and related topics, no text, no matter how well written, can substitute for professional hands-on instruction. These materials should be used for academic study only.

Printed in the USA

In memory of my father, Dr. Robt. (Bob) Kerr, and Robbie Kerr,
my loving brother.
I miss you both.

ACKNOWLEDGMENTS

There are many people I am grateful to know who have supported and inspired me to write this book and launch Defense Kinetics, most of whom are my many longtime students, who this book is dedicated to. I would especially like to thank Zach Bernotas for his countless hours participating in both photo and video shoots for the book and training resources. The love and support of all my family has been a blessing, especially from my wife, Serena, and my boys, Nick, Brett, and Adam. I'd also like to express my sincere appreciation to the many friends and experts who contributed their time and professional knowledge to the manuscript, including Kathy Ford, Jonathan Vogel, Rodney and Laura Lawrence, Sam King, Patrick O'Connor, Rob Neithart, Tamara Neiman, Armando Zatarain, and Chris Yo M.D., PhD.

Finally, writing a book is harder than I had expected and more rewarding than I could have ever imagined. None of this would have been made possible without my friend, co-author, and business partner, Luke Strockis. Both his and co-author Harrison Lebowitz's countless hours of collaboration, research, interviews, and writing talents made this book a reality. My sincere thanks to them and everyone in this acknowledgment.

CONTENTS

Foreword by Eric Cadena   xi

Use of Pronouns   xvii

Introduction - Snakes, Spiders, and Strangers at My House: The Evolution of Inside-Out Self-Protection   1

PART I
THE INSIDE SPHERE

1. Awareness Of Your Environment   15
2. Awareness of Individuals   61
3. Self-Awareness   91
4. Manging Daily Stress And Ego Through Mindfulness   107

PART II
THE OUTSIDE SPHERE OF SELF-PROTECTION

5. The Law Of Self-Defense   125
6. Comparing Martial Arts & Self-Protection Systems   145
7. Techniques To Deliver Pain, Defend, Or Escape   169
8. Weapons   247
9. Coming To The Aid Of Others   261
10. Intimate Partner Violence   269

PART III
WHEN TO ENGAGE

11. Response Calculus: Asking Yourself – What Would You Do?   283
12. The Parthian Shot   297

Endnotes   303
Bibliography   307
Index   309
About the Authors   313
Defense Kinetics   315

FOREWORD BY ERIC CADENA

Most of us haven't spent a lot of time thinking about brutality, much less how or if you would react in a moment when a serious threat to your life stood just a few feet away. Those things happen to other people in other neighborhoods. True, the knife-wielding psychopath-monster breaking into your house or apartment in the middle of the night is statistically rare. Far more common, however, are incidents of violence sparked by common, everyday encounters that escalate out of control, too often ending in tragedy. Alcohol, drugs, stress, anger, ego, and intolerance fuel most bloody confrontations in America, and they are almost always avoidable. This is violence born from stupidity, by those people who let substances or emotions magnify the slightest whiff of disrespect into a declaration of war and then respond with mindless brutality upon another human. Curiously, and in growing numbers, otherwise sane and reasonable people become idiots.

In between these idiots and the monsters of the world lie the criminals, predators, the desperately addicted, the vindictive, the jealous, and the mentally or emotionally unstable. The full spectrum of potential threats includes both people you know and complete strangers. They live in your neighborhood, eat and drink at your local restaurants and bars, travel on your same commuter train, and go to school with your kids. The idiot or the monster might even be you.

David Kerr's book, which is based on the philosophy that he developed in his studio, is the only one I know of that educates its readers on the most likely places, people, and encounters where violence may cross their path on any day, sometimes without warning, and teaches the strategy to spot trouble and the techniques for what to do about it. The book answers three critical questions we all should be familiar with:

How can I significantly improve my chances of avoiding violence in the first place?

If faced with a threating person or persons, how do I respond instantly with the most intelligent, practical, and lawful response?

When fighting to protect myself or loved ones from serious harm is unavoidable, how do I end the fight in a matter of seconds, regardless of size or strength?

For me, Kerr's system of Inside-Out Self-Protection isn't just a book about the benefits of awareness, mindfulness, or choosing a self-defense system. David Kerr's advice, training, love, and friendship literally saved my life, maybe just not in the way you might expect. The great Renaissance man

Dennis Prager once said, "The famous are rarely significant and the significant are rarely famous." And so, I suppose it is fitting that an unknown middle-aged man is writing the foreword to a book written by a significant man that few people have ever heard about outside of Southern California.

I was fortunate to enroll in David's studio at a time when my life was filled with deep personal struggles. These were my adolescent years. I was raised by a single mother, suffered from severe depression, and had an elaborate plan for ending it all. I suffered from uncontrollable bouts of crying that were triggered by the slightest provocation. I feared pain, was controlled by my feelings, and spent most of my young life living in the world of fantasy because reality was just too brutal. I had no friends and was bullied constantly. It goes without saying that girls weren't interested in me, and even if they had been, I lacked the confidence in myself to even initiate a conversation. Luckily, the studio's Inside-Out Self-Protection philosophy wasn't just about slaying dragons; it was also about conquering the demons that I had, that most of us have in some varying degrees, and that required a fearlessness that was unfamiliar to me at the time. The journey began with a lot of practice, sweat, humility, and moments of panic and self-doubt. What emerged was the confident and competent individual that had been locked away inside for so long.

David provided a vision, as he does in this book, through stories from his life, for the positive outcomes that can occur with proper training and action. At times this book will make you cringe (after all, it deals with the reality of violent scenarios), while at other times this book will make you laugh out loud at the idiotic things we do when we let our egos win out over common sense. To be sure, you will never look at Chinese food the same way! Most importantly, this book will challenge you as David challenged me. The end game was never just a different colored belt or sparring with a student just to see who was tougher. The end game comes from actual successes students experience in everyday life. His students include doctors, lawyers, retail clerks, police officers, insurance salespeople, businessmen and women, and high school and college students, who—over the years— have hundreds of these stories to share. After three years of training, I was applying the tools I learned for confronting complex confrontation scenarios in the streets to the many complex confrontations at work and in everyday life. One day, I too had my own story to share, and then I had another, and then another and then another.

I went on to become a respected high school teacher. I left that profession to serve my country honorably in Afghanistan as an Officer in the Army, where I taught many young men and women how to fight and survive using hand-to-hand fighting techniques that I had learned from David years earlier. I uprooted myself from Los Angeles and moved to Texas to work for a Fortune 50 company. I eventually found and married the love of my life, who happens to be a doctor. My closest friends are highly successful, decent people who say they love being around me. I could have never imagined this being my life as a frightened and confused nineteen-year-old. David played a significant role in my life story, and he is a major reason why hundreds of other men and women also have their own stories of survival and victory in their lives. I encourage you to begin your own journey with David, in the hopes that his book will give you the confidence to deal with any and all idiots or monsters, whether inside you or someone else, and who may one day knock at your door.

Eric Cadena
CPT. U.S. Army (Honorably Discharged)

USE OF PRONOUNS

Research over time has consistently shown that men are more likely to commit violent crimes than women. Today, over 90% of federal and state prisoners are men. According to 2017 FBI crime statistics, men perpetrated 97% of rapes, 90% of murders, 80% of all aggravated assaults and other violent crimes, and 70% of crimes against family or children. Men are also more likely than women to be victims of violence, but only very slightly, and certainly women are statistically victims of sexual assault in far greater numbers than men.

For these reasons, and to make this book easier to read, when explaining hypothetical encounters, I chose to use the form *he* exclusively when referring to the aggressor subject and *him* or *her* more equally when referring to the victim or potential victim of a violent act. For the actual violent encounters referenced in the book, the true names and sexes are used unless noted otherwise. This isn't a message to ignore women as potentially violent threats. There are brutally violent female inmates in our prisons, but statistically speaking, if you are unfortunate enough to be involved in a violent encounter, it most likely will involve a male aggressor.

David

INTRODUCTION

SNAKES, SPIDERS, AND STRANGERS AT MY HOUSE: THE EVOLUTION OF INSIDE-OUT SELF-PROTECTION

There are dozens of books written on self-defense, the fear of brutal criminals and crimes, or sophisticated weapons and response tactics, virtually all of them written by ex-Navy SEALS or former military intelligence officers, criminologists, or law enforcement agents. This isn't one of them, and I am none of the above. I'm David Kerr, an ordinary guy by most standards, who happens to have been involved in a lot of nasty fights.

After reading my story, you'll know why this book focuses on how to avoid violence in the first place, and if you can't avoid it or manage escape, how to survive it, but from a more practical point of view. I wrote this book for the average person—those who probably don't deal with violence as a profession and who haven't been formally trained to counter it. It's also for anyone who is unnerved—and perhaps feeling vulnerable—after reading near daily accounts of mass shootings and other violent crimes in the news, but who also refuses to let those anxieties prevent them from living their lives to the fullest.

Many of us live with these twin crocodiles of fear and invulnerability lurking just below the surface of our consciousness, and either one of them can be helpful or dangerous. After years of wading into uncertain waters with nothing attacking us, fear and vulnerability wanes. We rationalize away violent crime in the news media much the same way. If it's never happened to us or someone we know, it becomes a distant and abstract event that happens to other people in other neighborhoods. We go back to our daily routines while quietly convincing ourselves that "what happened to that unlucky person will never happen to me."

Or maybe you don't have that kind of air of invincibility around you, but instead you feel powerless, stressed, or overwhelmed by the very idea of confronting someone who—in your presence—may act irrational, aggressive, or violently. If so, you're not alone.

The American Psychological Association's latest Stress in America survey shows that fears over gun violence and sexual assault now rival the more typical worries about the economy, money, and work, especially for young adults. Startlingly, more than one-third of the survey participants reported personal safety as a significant source of stress in their lives, the highest in the survey's ten-year history.[1]

Now, more than ever, it's time to take control of your life, reduce your stress and anxiety, and be prepared to protect yourself from anyone looking to do you harm. The methodology I've developed doesn't come from any single fighting or self-defense system, be it military, law enforcement, boxing, or the martial arts. Rather, I've been influenced by all of them. I've drawn from my experience of decades of paid and unpaid encounters with idiots, violent people, and violent situations, some of them self-inflicted. What I am going to impart comes from studying and training in a wide variety of fighting systems and martial arts styles over the past 30 years to sort out the practical from the theatrical, and the enduring principles from the latest fads, meticulously shedding any concept or technique I was taught where its value to surviving a real-life violent encounter seemed solely for the reasons of institutional or cultural traditions, style points, egoism, or degree of difficulty. In other words, since my early teens, I've explored dozens of disciplines and have researched and tested hundreds of techniques, critically focusing on what would be most effective in a real-world setting. And I have distilled this vast amount of information and experience down to what I have taught my own self-protection students over the past two decades, with updates and improvements as necessary.

The information in this book will help you to avoid or survive a violent encounter, but without investing 30 years like me, or paying for and training in dozens of different boxing and martial arts courses to see what really works. This book is for anyone, regardless of gender, size, or self-protection experience, who wants to be more confident, make quicker, smarter choices under stress, and live their lives better prepared for a potential violent encounter, be it with the schoolyard bully, the drunk idiot, a predator, or the unimaginable moment of fighting for your life against a vicious and violent attacker—a monster.

I realize that learning effective strikes, kicks, and blocks for personal defense from a book has its limitations without the benefit of an instructor and practice partner. For this reason, I've limited the physical techniques in this book to one chapter of "essential" default skills that have proven to be effective yet easy to learn and execute (there are also video demonstrations available on the internet of each technique to aid in your training). Most of this book, therefore, focuses on how to improve your odds of never having to use these techniques to thwart an attack in the first place, which may have a lot more to do with you and the choices you make than you think. For all the news focused on senseless violence and random assaults, these incidents are statistically rare. More common are violent encounters that are avoidable, and where—too often—we, ourselves, become our own worst enemy.

Case in point, Steve, a Harvard-educated marketing consultant, has been a student of mine off and on for several years. He returns to the studio when time permits to brush up on past techniques and learn new ones. He's a gregarious, fit man in his 40's, of average height and weight. Recently, while walking out of a neighborhood liquor store, Steve was suddenly and violently struck from behind with a wine bottle across his head, just above the right temple. Two more strikes quickly followed to the left side of his skull. While covering his head, Steve lowered his center of gravity and turned toward the unseen assailant. From his crouched position, he proceeded to lunge at his attacker, planting his forearm across the assailant's chest, and driving his forward energy directly into him. The attacker, several inches taller and 40 pounds heavier, landed flat on his back, dropping the wine bottle in mid-air. When he opened his eyes, the stunned attacker saw Steve crouched over his chest and hip, hands in position and ready to pummel him. But Steve didn't have to. The attacker was so shocked at how fast the tables had turned on him that he froze. Bystanders called the police. Steve did everything right under the circumstances described—he used a cover and pivot move, followed by surprising his opponent with a technique I call "The Attacking Forearm." Steve even showed remarkable restraint by not retaliating against the man who had just seconds ago christened Steve's head with a nine-dollar bottle of Merlot. Steve did everything right, that is, except for Steve having escalated the situation that led up to the attack in the first place!

It turns out that Steve's 9:05 AM entrance into the liquor store to buy some smokes sent the liquor storeowner into a foul-mouthed tirade because the owner hadn't yet "turned on the lights." Though the door was unlocked and it was several minutes after the posted opening hours, the owner demanded Steve leave immediately, shouting more obscenities. Ignoring the demands, Steve sauntered over to the cooler case, pulled out a cold beer, and tossed it towards no one. As the beer bottle smashed on the floor, Steve calmly walked out the door, his back to the storeowner, waving his middle finger up in the air as a parting shot. Unbelievably, Steve never looked back to see if his own actions had drawn a response. Less than 25 feet out the door of the liquor store, Steve was clocked on the side of the head with a wine bottle with enough force that, if it had landed slightly lower across his temple, could have proven fatal.

On that day, Steve was his own worst enemy. A smart, successful man, who subjectively felt he was verbally attacked beyond reason, couldn't let it go, his ego now dictating his direction. Instead of leaving, perhaps with a reminder to the storeowner that he would take his business elsewhere from then on, Steve escalated the situation, which in turn, sent the storeowner into an adrenaline-infused rage, sparking a felony assault.

Walking away from mindless insults and juvenile behavior is difficult, especially for males; the temptation to "teach this guy a lesson" burns its way steadily down the fuse of perceived injustice until it explodes, prompting a response that (with a little luck) ends without an arrest, a lawsuit, serious injury to someone ... or worse. My advice is to be the better person, move on, and enjoy your day as planned. It's almost never worth the trouble it brings. Steve didn't take my advice—as demonstrated, he failed to implement one crucial element of my instruction that you will be reading about, the inside or internal training—and it could have killed him.

———

Looking the other way was a skill I was forced to acknowledge as useful at an early age. Born in San Gabriel, California, I was the son of a prominent doctor in the field of sports medicine, who performed a circumcision on *himself* and, on another occasion, recruited my very reluctant eight-year-old brother to be on the yanking end of a stubborn hemorrhoid my father had. It was his other eccentricities, however, that I credit for my early appreciation of awareness and respect for danger.

As a kid, my father regularly took my sister and me out to the desert to hunt rattlesnakes *for fun*. We had an Egyptian King Cobra, a 12-foot Python snake, and Ralph, a 160-pound gray wolf, as pets, along with a dozen exotic spiders, some poisonous. The latter would weave webs the size of manhole covers in the upper corners of our cellar, which doubled as our weightlifting room (it was just a matter of time before one of us iron-pumping kids would run into a territorial dispute with our eight-legged friends). And for reasons I wouldn't fully understand until years later, world famous martial artists, action movie heroes, elite athletes, and rock stars frequently visited our house. It was awesome, until my father, Dr. Robert Kerr, started receiving death threats in 1984 directly related to his unique medical practice. Day and night found strangers in cars parked in front of our house. I was only 14 years old, but it seemed like a good time to learn self-defense.

Yet, if not for my father's profession, I never would have met my first real mentor—Bill Laich. Bill was a U.S. born M.D./PhD. practicing in Europe. He wanted to learn the finer aspects of sports medicine from my dad, who invited Bill to live with us for the next two years. Bill was a 5th degree black belt (11th degree now) in Shotokan, a very popular Okinawan system of karate. While I enjoyed playing sports, especially football, I didn't know much about karate at the time, beyond Chuck Norris movies. Bill became a father-like figure and the catalyst for my interest in martial arts. Bill exposed me to Shotokan. He showed me how incredibly effective and intense Shotokan karate was, and his confidence was overwhelming, which I loved, and so I began to train with Bill.

As I was growing up, the community of San Gabriel was growing and changing too. You could find everything from million-dollar homes to street gangs in the quickly expanding and diverse neighborhoods of tree-lined streets where we roamed. I witnessed several gang fights, one with a fatality. The fights were fast and violent, and involved no martial arts, just heavy-handed punches. They were the exact opposite of the coordinated, controlled fights of Shotokan. Gangbangers didn't fight pretty, but they fought effectively, and I wanted to know why and how. It was the beginning of my life-long passion to learn the strengths and weaknesses of all the best-known fighting systems, from western style boxing to Muay Thai, Wing Chun, Judo, Jiu-Jitsu, Jeet Kune Do, and others. I put years of this diverse training to the test, as I was involved in literally hundreds of fights working as a bouncer for five years while attending college and playing football for the University of Southern California. My fighting and control techniques as a bouncer caught the eye of some local law enforcement officials who asked me to train them in my spare time. They were among the first of hundreds of students I began to train, and to learn from as well.

Today, I teach simple methods derived from each of these

fighting systems, all designed for one purpose: inflicting devastating pain and injury on a would-be attacker. My students are people just like you, and they find these methods extremely effective regardless of their size or strength. While I'll share with you some of the physical techniques from the courses I teach, equally important, I'll teach you something most other self-protection instructors fail to teach: the understanding that true self-protection always starts from the inside out. Put the kicks, strikes, and eye jabs aside for a moment. A key aspect to "Inside-Out" personal defense is the understanding that many of the situations that can lead to poor outcomes are avoidable. As you'll see, the "Inside-Out" personal defense is and should be your very first and most important line of defense. You can avoid most violent crime around because you are the one who controls your actions and reactions to virtually all situations in your life.

Another essential ingredient of "Inside-Out" personal defense is having the proper mindset. Developing the proper mindset and attitude in your life, along with the activities you choose to participate in, will absolutely dictate your response to a violent situation or help you to avoid it altogether. As we'll explore, we don't need to have the mentalities or the training of combat soldiers or police officers to face the world around us. Still, when no other choice exists, we need to be equipped with the mindset to react without hesitation and with controlled violence to a person looking to cause us serious harm, and we need the skills to respond with reasonable force to less lethal attacks, which is to say, only that force necessary to stop an idiot or assailant from attacking. By the time you finish this book, if unavoidable crime or aggression crosses your path, you will have that mindset and you will know what to do at "go time." And all of this leads to true confidence and a surprising sense of well-being.

PART I

THE INSIDE SPHERE

Again, I term my methodology of self-protection, "*Inside-Out Self-Protection.*" The "*outside*" sphere of the personal defense refers to the physical responses (run, hide, fight) to the instructions received from your brain when a threat is upon you. When, indeed, fighting for your safety or survival, it relates to the specific precepts and techniques you'll learn to attack, defend, and defeat a threat. This is covered in Part Two of the book. Regarding the "*inside*" aspect of the personal defense, I'm talking about your mindset and intuition: what your brain does every day to keep you safe, and training your brain to be your ultimate sentry or protector. Untrained, the brain can short-circuit, freeze up, and fail you when you need it the most. Similarly, intuition—the gut reaction we have when "something doesn't feel right"—is a very powerful sense, but it's often dismissed when we just as quickly attribute these feelings to being overly cautious or even self-conscious about coming across as unfriendly or rude.

But why do we need my method of personal defense, or any method of personal defense? Well, once, in the 1980s, the Bureau of Justice Statistics tried to quantify the "lifetime likelihood of victimization" and determined that 83% of Americans could expect to be a victim of an attempted robbery, rape, or assault at least once as an adult. True, the study looked at the crime rate from 1975 to 1984, which were noted as high crime years, and variable risk factors exist that can increase or decrease your odds; I will be discussing risk factors—some of which are within your control, others not—in detail later. Regardless, FBI statistics revealed an estimated 1,247,000 violent crimes in the United States in 2017 alone, an increase of nearly 8.5% since 2014. In the same year, hate crimes—those motivated by race, ethnicity, religion, or sexual orientation—leaped by 17%. Isn't it worth it to lessen your own personal odds of being victimized?

Let's start with the *inside*.

Your "*inside*" training is all about your *mindset*, which is having an established set of attitudes toward protecting your-self and the will to act, a subject most people rarely even think about until something bad happens to them or someone they know. Simply stated, *mindset* is synonymous with awareness, plus action.

More than half of my new students enroll in my personal protection courses as a response to a violent threat or circumstance that personally affected them. The rest enrolled to be proactive; preparing before something happens to them. In either case, developing the proper mindset or awareness is essential for everyone and includes three critical components:

AWARENESS OF THE ENVIRONMENT
A heightened sense of your environment to best avoid violence.

AWARENESS OF OTHER INDIVIDUALS
A heightened sense of others who may pose a danger.

AWARENESS OF SELF
A heightened self-awareness and intuition to enable smarter decisions on multiple fronts and, when escape is not an option, to provide the confidence and will to respond to serious threats, often requiring split-second decision-making and sometimes inflicting brutal violence.

Let's take an in-depth look at these three components of awareness.

1

AWARENESS OF YOUR ENVIRONMENT

As crazy as it sounds, the snake hunting my father loved to do with my sister and me when we were kids did teach me some valuable lessons. I never stuck my hand in a dark hole, I learned to look at the ground three to four feet all around me as I walked to avoid stepping on one, and I knew that the hotter the weather, the more snakes would be slithering about. Rattlesnakes have three self-defense mechanisms: one is to use their camouflage to hide, another is to run away, and the third, if they feel like they're in danger, is to rattle, which means they're ready to strike if necessary. Being aware of the environment around me kept me safe, despite deliberately wandering into a dangerous landscape.

Years later, in my mid-teens, I noticed unusual nighttime activity across the street from my house, which was adjacent to a country club. Street parking was common because of the golf course, but after sunset, there was no golfing and no legitimate reason to be sitting alone in a parked car outside my house. Nevertheless, for weeks on end there would be strange cars with strange people sitting behind their wheels, sometimes seemingly waiting to be noticed, then driving off. I brought it to the attention of my dad early on. He brushed aside my concerns and told me not to worry about it, but my brother and I pressed him on it until he admitted that he had received "a few death threats." A few? To this day, I'm not sure if the rotating men in the parked cars outside our house were there to intimidate us or protect us, but newspaper stories at the time began to fill in some of the details.

In 1984, Los Angeles was the host city for the Summer Olympics. The use of anabolic steroids among athletes to improve muscle and enhance performance had become pervasive and insidious. My father literally wrote the book on anabolic steroids for athletes.[2] In his book, he revealed that his patients included more than 4,000 athletes from 20 countries. In my father's defense, this was a time before the dangers of steroid use were fully known. But he had begun prescribing these drugs, especially to athletes, because he was concerned about what they were purchasing on the black market. He later stopped prescribing these drugs because his patients continued to make purchases beyond and regardless of his prescriptions.

He was interviewed by Morley Safer on the television news program *60 Minutes* and was featured in a 1983 *Sports Illustrated* article on the controversy of anabolic steroids in amateur and professional sports. International politicians and sports associations began demanding to know the scope of steroid use and the names of athletes using them. A panel of Canadian investigators asked my father to testify about the subject and the participants. Unfortunately, some of his patients, fearing the possibility of being exposed, began threatening our family. It turns out elite athletes weren't the only ones fearful of being exposed for using anabolic steroids. Some of the biggest names in Hollywood action movies at the time were patients of my father, seeking to bulk up for their big screen performances with the aid of anabolic steroids. My dad, Dr. Robert Kerr, also a general practitioner, had an office just blocks away from our house, but celebrities and professional athletes were reluctant to visit his modest office in San Gabriel and share a waiting room with the locals, who almost certainly would have wondered out loud why a steady stream of global superstars would travel all the way to the San Gabriel Valley for a checkup from a seemingly small town doctor.

Instead, my father treated them at our house, which is how I ended up growing up with Hollywood action heroes and premiere Olympic and professional athletes hanging around my living room. And, while it wasn't unheard of to occasionally see a famous person in the city of San Gabriel (about an hour's drive east of Santa Monica or Brentwood, where many of them lived), it would have been highly unusual to see a parade of celebrities walking in and out of my father's medical office, and it's precisely this disconnection from the local norm that is at the heart of environmental awareness.

Environmental awareness is nothing more than your mind's recognition that various environments where you roam (train stations, shopping malls, your work place, college parties, sporting events, school, the gym, home, etc.)

usually include people dressed and acting in familiar and predictable ways, and doing and saying fairly "normal" things for the circumstances. A man in a trench coat in 100-degree heat at the hotel pool isn't normal, no more than a woman in a bikini would be on the subway. Both would be out of context from the baseline: the typical dress or behavior for the environment. It's also, however, the awareness that different environments pose unique threats to you and to me. Certain businesses, neighborhoods, and transit centers act as anchor points for criminal activity, or sometimes riskier environments are riskier simply because they're popular gathering places, like bars and clubs, where often a heavy amount of drinking occurs, frequently mixed with a couple of shots of ego and stupidity.

———

One critical aspect of self-protection is developing a personal defense mindset, which requires sharpening your awareness of the environment around you. Using a baseline context (normal activity for the situation) as a mental reference point speeds your ability to instantly recognize a potentially serious situation. In the fascinating book LEFT OF BANG, authors Patrick Van Horne and Jason A. Riley provide extensive detail on how the United States Marine Corps is training combat soldiers in new methods for patrolling villages and cities which are considered high-risk deployments in the Middle East and elsewhere. The term "left of bang" refers to activities a patrol will carry out *before* an enemy ambush or a suicide bomber attacks: the observations of people, places, and patterns that may tip the hand of the enemy's impending attack and prevent loss of life. In contrast, "right of bang" is the post-event intelligence gathering used to assess how the bomb or ambush might be thwarted in the future.

One specific observation tool in the new training teaches Marines to profile individuals as part of the overall awareness assessment. The authors are quick to point out, however, that the profiling taught by the Marines is different than the controversial and, for law enforcement, illegal practice of profiling suspects based on race, commonly called "racial profiling." Instead of using profiling to identify and detain people who look like they don't belong in the neighborhood—for example, based on the color of their skin—the Marine's "Combat Hunter" profiling is far more comprehensive, including biometric indicators (uncontrollable, automatic, and observable reactions that people experience under stress), in addition to spotting secretive behaviors, or a shifting demeanor out of sync with the baseline norms for the environment. The practical application of this deeper level of awareness for keeping us safe in our own communities is apparent.

Quite simply, if someone's behavior or clothing (for example, an oversized backpack) is oddly out of place for the environment you're in, take notice. It may be nothing, or it may be a clue that something may unfold at any moment, right in front of you. Just by acknowledging the abnormality, you stand a better chance of acting if necessary, seconds before anyone else around you can process that something or someone nearby is a threat to his or her life. It's not likely to be as obvious as a man wearing a trench coat at the pool in

100-degree heat, but it's often less subtle than you might think. Too often, however, we are reluctant to trust our intuition and act on it.

Let's take a more comprehensive look at threats that are commonly associated with specific environments: places you and I may frequently be found. I'll also suggest some strategies for avoiding a violent encounter in these environments and for rehearsing your *response calculus*, which is that quick calculation your brain needs to make in choosing the best course of action under the circumstances.

VIOLENCE IN THE HOME

For many of us, our home—and our neighborhood—is the environment in which we spend most of our time. It is also where home invasion, sexual assault, and intimate partner violence (domestic violence) is more likely to occur. If you live in a high crime neighborhood, drug buyers and sellers, panhandlers, and street gangs might also be threats, but the fear of a stranger sneaking into your home and doing harm to you or your children is, for many of us, our worst nightmare.

When it comes to home invasions, regardless of our neighborhood, most homes are burglarized during the day when the perpetrators have observed or guessed we're at work or school, not home. Yes, we feel violated and we need to deal with cleaning up the mess, the insurance company, and the police, but when a break in occurs when we're not around, we aren't in any personal danger, and danger is our topic of conversation. So, let's focus on self-protection in your home when you are *at home*. Beyond the obvious like locking doors and windows, consider investing in at least two things: a dog and a baton. (My father had exotic poisonous snakes and spiders for pets, but I don't recommend either one of these solutions for home protection ... they are not very trainable!) The dog, however, will often give you a heads-up bark 10-15 seconds before you'll ever hear anything strange, and the baton is an inexpensive, easy-to-use, effective weapon you can stash right by your bed (more on batons in the chapter on weapons).

Let's also keep things in perspective. Home invasions that result in homicides, where someone is murdered during a burglary, are exceedingly rare. The FBI reports that out of the 15,129 total murders nationwide in 2017, only 90 were related to burglary (.006%), and of those, one-third were committed by someone the victim knew. Of course, that statistic means nothing if you know someone who was murdered in their home. Nevertheless, if some stranger breaks into or enters your home in the middle of the night, it's almost never for your jewelry alone. Criminals brazen enough to enter your home when they know there's a high probability you are inside either get a thrill from the surprise, or they simply don't care if they're seen and confronted. Either way, it's not good. This is the worst type of predator. Grab your baton (or weapon of choice) and call 911. Even if you can't speak to the operator without tipping off your whereabouts to the intruder, the 911 dispatcher will use global position tracking or caller identification to send help. In many cities, you can even send a text to 911. Some experts recommend building or converting a room to a so-called "safe room," a super secure, windowless hideout designed just for the occasion of a home invasion. Let's be real, this isn't a practical solution for most of us.

If you're awakened by a home invader and can't escape, lock the bedroom door and position yourself against the wall just inside the door to the room. If the intruder enters, use your baton to bash the first body parts to show themselves. The shins or knees are excellent first strike targets, along with the side of the head, and these are likely to be the first body parts that cross the threshold. If the first thing you see is a weapon, attack and crush the hand or wrist holding the weapon. Follow up with repeated strikes to the side of the head, neck, collarbone, or ribs until there is no fight back from the intruder. Escape immediately and call 911.

I'm often asked why you shouldn't just turn on all the house lights to frighten the intruder into running away. The answer depends on whether the stranger is outside of or inside your house. If outside of, turning on lots of lights and making noise is an obvious deterrent. However, as I explained previously, any intruder in your home in the middle of the night isn't likely there to steal the cash in your cookie jar. Burglars interested in valuables hit your home when they're reasonably certain no one is there. By turning on the lights, you've illuminated the path to all bedrooms, made visible the family members in the home, and given up the crucial element of surprise. It's possible, of course, that the intruder is there only to seek money, electronics, or jewelry, and maybe the criminal calculated incorrectly that you were away on vacation and the house was empty. A flood of lights in this instance may scare them out of the house. Is it worth the risk to find out? What if they are there instead to rape or kidnap?

If you have children present during a late-night home invasion, I want to share with you some advice that may be counter-intuitive and perhaps controversial to you as a parent (as I am). If you're unable to contact the police, but can escape and seek assistance from a neighbor or a passing car, escape immediately and get help. There's a chance that by the time the home invader discovers you're gone, the police are already on their way. It changes the intruder's plans when he finds out there is no adult present in the home when there should be. He now must make a quick decision: stay and risk getting caught, or leave quickly. If the thought of abandoning your children while you flee to seek help is morally unacceptable, consider the odds of things turning out just fine if you don't get help fast. He's in your house in the middle of the night for a reason, and it's not likely to pilfer priceless artwork. Further, this is not the type of criminal that has any ethics or reason to negotiate. Think about the prospect of your children being tied up and forced to watch as you are sexually assaulted. Think about yourself being tied up and forced to watch one or more of your children being sexually violated. It's unspeakable, and it's also not likely that the anti-social predator is going to intentionally leave any witnesses alive to identify him. This is no time to worry about what your kids might momentarily think of you for escaping. All that matters are that you and your children are unharmed and live to see another day. [3]

Finally, on the topics of violence in your home from an abusive spouse or gang activity in the neighborhood, while this violence often takes place in and around the home, both are discussed elsewhere in the book, arguably because they are more complicated issues than simply being aware of your environment alone.

MASS TRANSIT—CRIME & CONFRONTATION

Mass transit stations are growing magnets for crime. A study of San Francisco's Bay Area Mass Transit (BART) train system revealed that nearly 80,000 incidents of crime were reported in 2013 alone, up 8% over the previous year and a 17% increase over the previous four years. Most involved larceny, burglary, and robbery (57%), followed by assault (13%), with drugs and vandalism similarly ranked at about 8% each.

Most of the crime happens within 150 feet of the transit center. Why? Several factors contribute to making transit centers one of the most popular and efficient areas for criminals to operate. They tend to be confined spaces that offer cheap and easy access, with crowds that include all walks of life, allowing criminals to blend in without notice. Transit centers also tend to operate day and night. Criminals feed off the steady, predictable stream of suitable targets and a relatively light police presence.[4]

That said, however, the most dangerous scenario is not at the station, but once you're on a moving train, plane, or bus. You're in an especially confined setting with no immediate opportunity to escape. Your options when faced with potential danger in this circumstance narrow considerably. Think about it, if you're seriously threatened, or come to the aid of someone being threatened, neither running nor hiding are strong options on a moving mass transit vehicle or aircraft.

If you encounter an individual who is shouting threats your way or at an innocent passenger, your best move is to bark two or three short, loud, and clear commands at the person for all in the vehicle to hear:

STOP!

GET BACK!

SIT DOWN!

SHUT UP!

DON'T TOUCH ME!

Don't negotiate a response, elaborate on the reasoning for your instructions, or mumble under your breath how crazy the world has become. Never beg or plead either, as criminals tend to prey on weakness. Keeping the commands very brief and clear keeps you from stumbling over your words while adrenaline is flooding your mind and body, and when directed at anyone hostile or intoxicated, are more easily processed and understood by them. As will be discussed later, if the threat doesn't immediately back down, or the threat moves towards you (into your six-foot "attack zone" as discussed in a moment), your inability to escape demands that you MUST attack first with an appropriate level of violence. "Appropriate" is enough physical violence to stop the threat and nothing more. The linear and compact striking techniques found in the martial art Wing Chun are highly effective for smaller, lighter people, and ideal for altercations in close quarters, such as the narrow aisles in trains, airplanes, and buses, and they are a significant influence in my self-protection system. Several Wing Chun strikes are demonstrated in the techniques chapter of this book. In the meantime, if you find yourself on a Metro bus up against a potentially violent threat, a good old-fashioned tackle is also a good option; the aggressor won't be expecting it and others are around to assist after the proactive attack, if needed.

Regardless, never forget this next piece of advice in any encounter:

> *Always assume the person has one or more concealed weapons. Never let the threatening person reach into their pockets or behind their back or under their pant cuffs.*

Instruct other passengers to assist in restraining the threat until you arrive at the next stop and the police are on the scene.

Since I just mentioned the term "attack zone," and will reference it again before you get to the chapter on techniques for delivering pain, blocks, and escapes, here is a quick explanation of what I want you to know. Your attack zone is the distance between you and the threatening person, which should be no less than about six feet, or roughly the height of the potential attacker. Experienced students and experts can get away with a greater distance than six feet from the threatening person because they have been trained to attack with an unusually long attack step. In other words, they can strike, choke, or take down a threat in a split second using a single step. If you are inexperienced or significantly shorter in height than the aggressor, you may need to tighten your attack zone to as little as five-feet to maintain sufficient power and momentum in the event that you need to execute a preemptive combination of strikes. The attack zone is not just for calculating the distance you need in order to strike your opponent first with a single step—it's also your buffer zone. It provides you with time to react to the aggressor should he move toward you first, whether it be to escape, block his incoming punch, counter an attempt to tackle or grab you, or attack and disarm a weapon that suddenly appears.

The critical takeaway for the attack zone is to *never* let any threatening person move closer to you than the five or six feet. Doing so allows the bad guy to strike or stab YOU with a single step and reduces your reaction time to escape or defend yourself. There's nothing wrong with taking a step or a step-and-a-half back to create the space you need, but stepping back further increases your chances of tripping on something unexpectedly.

PARKING LOTS

Parking lots are a popular playground for criminals and predators, and they are a particularly dangerous environment. Parking garages provide plenty of dark places for criminals to hide—be it in staircases, between cars, or simply in the shadows. Similarly, outdoor lots attract crime particularly at night, especially if not well lighted. Here are a few suggestions to avoid problems:

- If shopping, have a clear view to the store entrance.
- Look behind you and inside your car before you enter.
- Don't wear ear buds or talk on your cell phone.
- If it's late, quiet, or your intuition senses something, call mall or campus security for an escort.
- If you're approached for assistance from a stranger, let them know you will alert parking management of their situation on your way out of the lot. Don't offer a ride to any stranger.
- If you're close enough to your car and someone is acting suspicious, use your ignition key's emergency button to set off your car alarm, bringing unwanted noise and flashing lights.

ROADWAYS

On the road, you might encounter people and situations that differ from your ordinary experiences and acquaintances. Yet, most of us spend a lot of time in our cars, so I thought it beneficial to have a brief discussion of the risks. After all, you can be comfortably cruising along, listening to your favorite music on your way to work or shopping, assuming you are in a safe place and, in an instant, have your world turned into a nightmare.

The risks on the roadways hide in surprisingly common situations:

- Your car breaks down
- Another traveler signals for assistance
- You're involved in an accident

Of course, road rage is another, and unfortunately growing threat to motorists on the highways, so much so that I've devoted a section to it in the next chapter. That leaves us remaining with circumstances mostly requiring the use of common sense. But let's review the "common sense" part because, unfortunately, it's anything but common. If car trouble forces you to the side of the road, lock your doors and call for assistance. Wait until the authorized tow truck arrives. If a passerby stops and asks if you need assistance, politely refuse and let them know help is arriving in a minute.

Most robberies (taking valuables by force, threat, or violence) occur on roads and highways more than any other location. If you see someone else on the side of the road flagging you down for assistance, slow down and signal to them via hand gestures that you are calling for assistance. If you're concerned for their safety, pull to the roadside 100 yards from their disabled vehicle (preferably behind the car for a better view of activities), put on your flashers, and wait until assistance arrives. The self-protection mindset here is to remain vigilant. This is your safest course of action because things are not always as they appear, regardless of what you think you see. Simply use common sense.

SPORTING EVENTS AND CONCERTS

It's an unfortunate sign of the times when the 60th Annual Grammy Awards featured a special performance paying tribute to victims of gun violence and terrorism at live music events. The deadliest mass shooting in U.S. history to date occurred at one such event: the sniper at the Route 91 Harvest Festival in Las Vegas in October 2017 left 58 dead and almost 500 injured in his wake. Earlier that same year, terrorists targeted an Ariana Grande concert in Manchester, England. The bombing left 23 dead and over 500 injured. This attack, along with a bombing outside a soccer stadium during terrorist attacks in Paris in 2015, brought home the message that it's not just about security at the actual concert venue anymore, but the surrounding area as well. Keeping concertgoers safe has become a larger and more complicated task for law enforcement and security staff, all of which makes it that much more important that you take a personal stake in your own well-being.

Fortunately, mass shootings and terrorist attacks at event venues are rare (although it may not seem like it from watching the news). Your chances of victimization by violence at a concert or sporting event are far greater coming from a fellow concertgoer or sports fan than from a mass shooter or terrorist bomber, and in most cases, alcohol consumption plays a significant role in the violence.

If you've ever walked from your car or a pregame tailgate party to the entrance of an NFL or college football stadium, you know the kind of buzz that's in the air—the bigger the game, the greater the energy, with thousands of fans that have devoted hours of time into their liquid, pregame preparation. Dressing in your favorite player's jersey may be all it takes to get an earful of attitude from an opposing team's fans, most of it good-natured, but some of it from idiots who hope to bait you into reacting. Unless the person physically touches you, throws something at you, or threatens your wife or kids, ignore the drunken rants and keep walking to the stadium. Report the incident to stadium security. But if you're on your way into the game and are physically threatened, remember, the punk that grabbed your team hat off your head or threw a beer at you didn't come to the game by himself. You need to be aware of who his buddies are and not let yourself get tied up in a fight where you make it easy to get sucker punched. If you genuinely feel in danger of imminent and serious bodily harm, quickly assess who is nearby, and then proactively deliver a quick flurry of pain to the troublemaker. Maintain a mindset that others might choose to intervene on behalf of the idiot who threatened you. Do everything you can to:

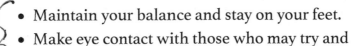

- Maintain your balance and stay on your feet.
- Make eye contact with those who may try and challenge you.

If his buddies are aware that their "friend" was the instigator and you quickly put down the idiot in a groaning heap on the grass, chances are very good they'll want nothing to do with fighting you. And for God's sake, don't forget to get your hat back!

If you're at your seat in the stadium and you find the situation intolerable, I would strongly suggest that you avoid an altercation unless it's impossible to do so. Stadiums breed a mob mentality fueled by alcohol, none of which leads to anything good. The narrow rows alone have contributed to many busted legs. Instead, locate the nearest usher or security personnel. Many stadiums now provide you with a number to call or text for just such a circumstance; put it in your phone before the event and use it if needed. Given the cost of tickets and parking, physically engaging with an unruly fan is a sure-fire way to get ejected from the event and possibly spend the night in jail. A waste of money and time.

How is this different than the same kind of serious threat outside of the stadium? To begin with, inside the venue, you have almost immediate access to ushers, police, or security staff to assist you. The police and the courts would reasonably expect you to ask for available assistance if time permitted. But half a mile away, in the parking lot's jam-packed tailgate section, quick access to security is unlikely, or uncertain at best. Also, from a self-defense tactical standpoint, you're on level ground and unrestricted by stadium seats and tiny aisles. In contrast, defending yourself from your Row 57, Seat 118, Upper General Admissions Sky Seat requires you to fight like a trapped animal on the edge of a cliff. Engaging someone in the stadium seats is a recipe for injury, ejection, arrest, and litigation.

Most things worth doing have risks involved, but that doesn't mean one shouldn't do them. Live concerts and sporting events, despite traffic and some unruly fans, can be amazing experiences that you shouldn't avoid just because they may be riskier than staying home. Nevertheless, you need to understand the risks, especially considering current events. Knowing what to do to protect yourself and your loved ones if an attack (or earthquake or fire) occurs at the venue you are visiting is more important than ever.

Prior to the event, review the seating chart and familiarize yourself with the layout of the venue and the location of your seat. You may want to download the chart to your phone. You can also do a search online to see if the event or performers have been a target of violent threats and check the venue's website for any posted information about security efforts being undertaken at the venue. It's always a good idea to formulate a game plan with your party in the event of an emergency: What will you do? How will you communicate? Where will you go? Upon arrival at the venue, locate the emergency exit closest to your seat—just like on an airplane—and take note of where event staff or security/police officers are posted. If you see someone acting strangely or in a way that makes you uncomfortable, notify event staff or security.

———

If you hear gunfire, take cover until you can identify the general direction of where the gunfire is coming from. And just a quick note about gunfire and sound: determining with certainty from which direction shots are being fired can be tricky in certain environments because of the acoustics. Listen carefully, make your best judgment about the direction of the gunfire, and run at a brisk pace in the opposite direction of the gunfire or bomb blast. Running at full speed when you are panicked is difficult without stumbling, because your brain has redirected blood flow from your appendages to your vital organs. Run at 80%. Stay low and away from glass that could shatter. If you get caught up in a stampede, move away from the center of the mob and grab onto a wall or pillar for safety. If you find yourself in the shooter's line of fire, take cover behind a solid barrier (tree, steel trash bin, car, concrete pillar) until his pause for reloading allows you an opportunity to run even farther away to another barrier.

It may seem ridiculously obvious to say this, but the greater the distance from the shooter, the more difficult it is for him to fatally shoot you. Within five feet of the shooter, there's a 53% chance of being killed by the gunfire. At 50-feet, the chances of being killed drop to 6%. [5]

If there's an armed attack and you can't escape quickly or in the direction of safety, look for an open door, perhaps behind a concession stand, storage room, or offices. Lock the door, turn out the lights, and stay silent. If the attacker needs to make an extra effort to get into a room, he will hopefully move on. Still, don't rely on hope alone. Stay behind or adjacent to the door and be ready to attack the shooter's weapon if he enters the room. If you're in a group, get coordinated for a simultaneous ambush on the shooter's weapon and the shooter.

Teens and Concerts

While teenagers relish the live gigs and concert-crowd experience, parents have some homework to do to make informed choices and increase the odds of their children having a safe and positive experience. Depending on the venue and the artist, the concert scene presents concerns that range from a teen's physical safety to types of behaviors some parents would rather not have their children exposed to. In addition to drug and alcohol use, expect the unexpected, including mosh pits, physical assault, and sexual harassment. Only you know what is right for you and your teen, but here are some suggestions:

Confirm Designated and Alternative Meeting Places

These should be places outside the venue where you and your teen can gain access without a ticket. The alternative meeting place is used in the event of an emergency, where the main exit or meeting place may be impacted by an incident or jammed with people escaping a situation elsewhere in the venue.

Buddy System

Don't send your teen to an event alone. Have them bring a friend and insist they stick together. When one of them goes to the restroom or gets a snack, they both go. No exceptions.

ID and Contacts on Person

If your teen doesn't have a driver's license, have them keep an ID card (or take a picture of it and store it in their phone and yours), along with emergency contact information. Have the phone numbers for friends attending the show with your teen and their parents and vice versa.

Communication

Ask your teen to check in at least twice; the first time when they get to their seat, and again when the show is over. Encourage them not to be shy in asking venue staff for help or directions.

Stay Close as an Option

Consider having dinner near the concert venue and inform your teen of the name of the place and its location. Still not close enough for comfort? Buy a ticket for yourself. If you're just too worried about your teen and what might happen at the concert, go with them. Many venues that cater to teens now have designated waiting spaces inside for parents & guardians. So, go and hang out!

BARS & CLUBS

Years of being a bouncer at a variety of bars and clubs around Los Angeles gave me a sober, first-hand account of nightlife culture. And although not its purpose, it provided me with a great testing ground to see what techniques worked best in each circumstance. Most patrons were younger and enjoyed their evening out with friends without any problems. But unfortunately, I rarely worked a night without incident. Over the course of my bouncing career, I was probably involved in over 250 altercations, once taking down five guys. These were real fights, not just the two or three times a night when I had to physically remove someone from a bar. Not surprisingly, alcohol was almost always the key feature and the single biggest culprit behind rude, aggressive, or violent behavior.

Alcohol contributes to violence by limiting a drinker's perceived options during a conflict, heightening their emotions, increasing their willingness to take risks, reducing their fear of consequences, and impairing their ability to even recognize an escalating situation. The problems aren't limited to frequent heavy drinkers. Many of the "trouble-some" guests that bar staff, bouncers, and the police deal with are ordinary drinkers who go on binges, drinking more than they usually do or on empty stomachs. It's not just my own observations of the link between overconsumption and violence. Studies show, in general, those who drink exces-sively are more aggressive and are more likely to be seriously injured than those who drink moderately or not at all.[6]

A sure sign of general over serving occurring (and a signal to leave) is when you can't hear the person across the table from you speaking because of a sudden jump in the noise level of the customers. Additionally, staying until the establishment's mandatory closing hour is also asking for trouble. The looming last call encourages some patrons to drink heavily just before closing, knowing they can't legally buy another drink for the rest of the night. These customers are the ones most likely to get aggressive, which is why bars with later closing hours experience more assaults than those with standard business hours. Additionally, if you're in an area with a high concentration of bars and all bars close at the same time, the risks of conflict outside the bars and on the surrounding streets increase significantly.

———

The employees and security personnel of an establishment can be a reliable predictor of its safety for guests. They reflect the attitude, professionalism, and quality of training provided by the ownership, or an indication that the ownership is absent or not engaged. An unfriendly, confrontational, and aggressive staff can set the tone in bars, pubs, and nightclubs, unintentionally encouraging patrons to engage in aggressive or violent behavior. A bouncer's very presence may subconsciously signal to some patrons that physical confrontation and force are acceptable ways to resolve disputes in that bar. One of the reasons club and bar owners frequently hired me or provided me with referrals to other clubs is because I understood that too often, the bouncers were more of the problem than the guests. Unlike other bouncers, whose default was an immediate physical response, I honed an ability to assess a situation in advance.

I became a student in the study of patrons and recognizing the troublesome element. I knew exactly who was going to be problematic and could often defuse the situation in advance of any issues arising. These individuals would come in displaying an over-the-top amount of intensity— and anger—rather than being in some sort of relaxed state. I could tell from their demeanor and attitude that they were just looking for a fight, especially if they'd brought a female friend to the bar. Someone simply looking at them or the person accompanying them would set them off. If you asked me, I'd attribute their abnormal reaction to ego and insecurity, but I wasn't being paid to be a closet psychologist. Anyway, I became so good at recognizing trouble before it happened that an L.A County Sheriff noticed my skills, handed me his card, and the next thing I knew, I was training twelve L.A. County Sheriffs.

Learning to deescalate potential conflicts, especially between patrons who have been drinking, is essential not only for the safety of the personnel who work at the bar, but for its reputation and financial success.

Some establishments employ professional security, but it's still the same issue. They can either be helpful in assisting the bar or club staff in dealing with over-served guests, or contribute to the problem. Some security staff see themselves as enforcers of the club's policies, irrespective of its immediate impact on customer safety. The more aggressively the security staff handles patrons, the more aggressively patrons respond. Like bouncers, many security employees have the muscle but lack the skills to defuse violence. Don't let the presence of uniformed security lull you into a false sense of safety. Be vigilant, drink in moderation, and leave if the vibe of the establishment doesn't feel right.

Bars seem especially designed for competitive situations, stirring up high emotions that arise whether patrons are watching sporting events on television or competing in pool, darts, or other bar games. And they are where, typically, young men gather and drink to bond or meet women. It doesn't take much for good times to turn into anger, frustration, or worse. Competition inside and outside the bar—for the attention of a busy bartender or an attractive patron, slow food service, packed standing or dancing space—any of these things can trigger tempers and violence.

Unfortunately, studies have shown that those who fight in bars are not deterred by negative consequences (such as minor injuries, tension among friends, or trouble with the police), all of which tend to be delayed consequences. The perceived rewards are more immediate and lead them to feel justified about fighting for a worthy cause, bolstering one's ego, increasing group cohesion among friends, getting attention, feeling powerful, and having entertaining stories to tell.[6]

Not that they necessarily deserve being assaulted, but some assault victims do precipitate the assault. How about the obnoxious guy that hits on your wife or girlfriend when he knows she's with you, or the guy who inappropriately grabs or touches a woman? Both instances deserve a response, but maybe not the one you want to hear. The guy hitting on your lady is a jerk, but you can take it as a compliment, and she can speak for herself when responding to him. On the other hand, them grabbing your wife, girlfriend, or partner is physical assault and may be sexual battery, depending on the state where you live. You have every right to call the police and file charges. However, if you choose instead to put your fist into his jaw (as tempting as it may be), leaving thirteen of his teeth on the marble floor and a blood-stained mop bucket for the police to photograph as evidence of battery, you have now put *yourself* at risk for charges as well. Keep in mind that security cameras are everywhere these days, and the video recordings will be one of the first things the police will ask management to hand over. Your best bet is to demand that the rude customer apologize to your date and insist that management throw him out of the establishment. It may not be as satisfying as a punch in the face, but I'm trying to keep you out of trouble.

Not all bar fights involve someone's girlfriend. In some neighborhood establishments, simply looking at someone the wrong way may trigger a violent reaction. One thing is predictable, however—the overwhelming majority of those involved in bar fights, both attackers and victims, are young men between the ages of 18 and 29 years old. And like the easy target criminal predators prefer, most victims of violence in and around bars and clubs tend to be vulnerable; they are usually smaller than their attackers, are either alone or in a small group, and are more drunk than their attackers.

If you're tempted to respond with violence to an aggressive or over-served idiot at a bar, consider this: he may be there with his buddies, and improvised weapons are everywhere, including bottles, glasses, heavy beer mugs and pitchers, pool cues, heavy ashtrays, and bar furniture. The more available these items are to the troublemaker and his comrades, the more likely the group is to use one against you, causing a potential serious injury which you may never see coming. Again, my advice: unless someone is trying to deliberately intimidate you with physical threats or actions (and not just running off at the mouth), gather your friends and head for another establishment. It's almost never worth it.

The Rape Drug Crisis

One thing has changed since my bouncing days in the 1990's: the rise in the use of club drugs, which has grown to epidemic proportions. Many club drugs, including rape drugs (such as Rohypnol), are used for criminal sexual purposes. Rohypnol and other rape drugs sedate a person similarly to alcohol, but more potently, and at the very least, make the target susceptible to influence. The criminal's goal is always the same: to convince the target to engage in sexual acts that they wouldn't otherwise have agreed to. In the worst-case scenario, rape drugs are used to make a person unconscious and unable to resist any sexual advance. Cases of women waking up in a stranger's bed with no memory of the night before are common. Even scarier, women may regain consciousness in an alley or other secluded location, having been left behind by their rapist. However, women aren't the only people who may fall victim to these drugs; men are also victimized and violated. That's why it's important for everyone who goes to bars, clubs, or parties to understand the pervasiveness of club drugs.

Club drugs are those drugs that are used in a party setting to enhance the experience, or in some instances, to influence other people's behaviors. They go by a variety of slang names, and I've listed them below for you. In some cases, people who take club drugs may grow aggressive towards others and get themselves into dangerous physical altercations. Club drugs often remove a person's sense of self-control, causing them to behave in irrational and risky ways, including the before-mentioned engaging in unwanted sex, driving too fast, or jumping from exceedingly high heights. However, even people who have no intention of taking club drugs may be at risk of drinking drug-laced liquor. Never leave your drink unattended. If you go to the restroom, bring it with you or have someone you trust watch it until you return. Don't accept a drink from a stranger if you didn't personally watch the bartender make it.

Another smart way to avoid club drugs is to understand what they are, what names they go by, and what they can do to you. Here is a summary of the most common club drugs, their slang names, and their physical and mental side effects:

Rohypnol – Commonly called "roofies," these substances are a benzodiazepine that works very quickly. These produce a variety of sedative effects, including dizziness, confusion, loss of control, anxiety, numbness, and even seizures. They are perhaps the most heavily used subset of club drugs known as "rape drugs," as they are often used to either cause a person to be susceptible to suggestion or to put them in a state of unconsciousness.

MDMA – Often known as Ecstasy, XTC, X, Adam, Clarity, and Lover's Speed, MDMA are typically taken in pill form and are very like amphetamines, causing a variety of effects. These include intense stimulation and even hallucinations. Effects can last up to six hours, with negative side effects such as confusion, paranoia, hypertension, dehydration, and anxiety.

GHB – Known as Grievous Bodily Harm, G, Liquid Ecstasy, or Georgia Home Boy, GHB is typically taken in liquid, powder, or tablet forms. Users often combine it with alcohol to increase its effects. It is a depressant that sedates the body and decreases self-control. It's often used as a "rape drug" or can even be used as a method to poison someone.

Ketamine – Commonly called Special K, K, Vitamin K, and Cat Valiums, Ketamine is an injection, liquid, or powder drug that causes effects not unlike PCP. This includes producing extreme energy, hallucinations, and a disconnection with reality. It can often result in psychotic breaks lasting for extended periods. It can also cause amnesia, high blood pressure, poor motor function, and even respiratory problems.

Methamphetamine – Also called Speed, Ice, Chalk, Meth, Crystal, Crank, Fire, and Glass. Unlike its sister drug, amphetamine, methamphetamine has no legitimate medical use. Instead, it is used to increase a person's energy to high levels by speeding up the body's own metabolism, causing a variety of dangerous symptoms, including heavy sweating, memory loss, aggression, mental damage, and even heart attacks.

LSD – Often called Acid, Boomers, and Yellow Sunshine, LSD causes severe hallucinations when ingested orally. It can cause a person to lose connection with reality in a dangerous way and may lead to temporary psychosis. Increased heart rate and blood pressure, as well as sleeplessness, are also common. "Flashbacks" to a hallucinatory state can occur years after the last use of LSD.

Despite whatever promises someone makes to you about the "desirable" effects of a club drug, ingesting it in a bar, club, or party setting is very risky. Take a pass and encourage your friends to do the same.

VIOLENCE IN SCHOOLS

Compulsory school attendance laws mean that a clear majority of children must leave the safety of their homes almost every day and enter a school building to interact with thousands of other kids coming from all kinds of homes. It's been this way for generations, and it's a natural part of the socialization process. What we see and read in the news, however, makes it feel like going to school has become a lot more dangerous than in the past. The truth is: it is and it isn't. On the positive side, the most recent survey conducted by the Centers for Disease Control (CDC) found incidents of adolescent fighting off campus were significantly down and fights on campus were slightly down. On the negative side, the study pointed to rapidly growing risks associated with mental health and sexual violence. So while schoolyard fights are trending down, physical assaults on other students, suicide, and sexual crimes are up. In the overall mix, the CDC study found incidents of bullying and intentional physical injury to students are as frequent as ever. Let's take a closer look at some of these.

Bullying

Officially, one in four public schools reported bullying occurred among students on a daily or weekly basis. My own hunch—from my years as a high school Dean of Discipline —is that these rates of bullying are much higher (and, yes, the Dean of Discipline does sound like a professional wrestler's name). As we know, bullying can occur in many environments, including cyberspace, but because it predominantly occurs in the school environment, I wanted to mention it here. I'll go into detail on bullying in the chapter *Awareness of Individuals* because the bully typically fits a certain type of individual, and again in the chapter *The Law of Self-Defense*, which explains what you can (and can't) do legally if you are the target of threats or actual violence from school bullies.

Mental Health

Our children live today in an increasingly anxious society. This anxiety, along with stress and depression, are all strongly linked to bullying, fighting, weapons on campus, a wide variety of high-risk behaviors, and mass school shootings. Anxiety disorders are the most common mental illness in America and roughly 30% of girls and 20% of boys (6.3 million school-age teens) have had anxiety disorders, according to data from the National Institute of Mental

Health. The issue has become so pervasive that *Time* magazine ran a cover story on the mental health of our children in 2016. The author, Susanna Schrobsdorff, reminds us that teen brains have always craved stimulation and teens' emotional reactions are by nature urgent and sometimes self-destructive. So, why is it different now? All of today's high school kids are the post 9/11 generation. They've never known a time when terrorism and school shootings didn't seem normal. They watched their parents struggle financially through a severe recession, and perhaps most importantly, they entered adolescence at a time when technology and social media were dramatically transforming society. Add to this frenzied mix the worry over how to pay for the cost of college as well as increased competition for top college admissions. The competitive nature of our schools and society, the lack of confidence in future job quality, or where the economy is headed are bound to bring on some sleepless nights for students and their parents. And as an overlay, we have the sheer hyper connectedness now possible through our smartphones, laptops, and streaming television, fueled by addicting social media sites, that have created a typhoon of stimulus that Schrobsdorff points out "we can't escape from, or don't know how."[7]

Today's youth spend less time sleeping, and less time in-person with their friends, while spending more and more time with their phones and digital media. We expect our youth to navigate this new storm of stimulus before many are mentally ready. The part of the human brain that translates emotion into logic isn't fully developed until age 25 or beyond, especially for boys. Yet, we flood our kids with expectations (often our expectations), along with quick remedies to stay on task. Today's young people—our future leaders, protectors, teachers, entrepreneurs, musicians, and factory workers—have access to more people, prescription drugs, and information than at any time in history, and it's overwhelming an entire generation. All of this has led to a growing sense of unhappiness among our youth. Some take their frustrations out on their parents or other students, in some instances turning to violence. Others, in growing numbers, take their own lives to escape the pain of anxiety and depression.

Sexual Assault in Schools

Violent crime in schools includes assault, particularly bullying, but also sexual assault in alarming numbers. This is true at both our nation's high schools and our college campuses.

> It's not a stranger that you need to worry about the most when it comes to sexual assault, but the person you know. [8]

Over 500,000 high school students say they have been coerced into sexual intercourse by their date, a jump of 30% in a four-year period. Another 385,000 students, according to the 2015 CDC survey, say they were *physically* forced into sexual intercourse. An astounding 20-25% of all women in college report they were sexually assaulted by physical force, violence, or incapacitation.

The college freshman experience of being away from

home for the first time can be both liberating and stressful (the same holds true for, say, a high school student at an unsupervised party), and women, especially, need to be extra cautious because they tend to be more likely the victims of sexual assault. Because of this, I devote the rest of this section to you. If you find yourself in a situation where guys are offering you free drinks, throw up an internal red flag of caution, and either insist on watching the drink being made, make the drink yourself, or politely decline the offer. Apart from the amount of alcohol a drink may contain (sometimes without the strong taste you would expect), date rape drugs are easy to slip into drinks. They are undetectable in the blood or urine stream the next day, and you'll have no memory of what happened. As mentioned before in the section on bars and clubs, if you choose to drink, don't leave your drink unattended. If you use the bathroom, bring your drink with you, or have a trustworthy friend watch your drink until you return.

Sexual Aggression

Alcohol or not, boys and men on dates who won't take "no" for an answer often look for any opportunity to justify their persistence. Be forceful and clear in expressing what you want. If a woman leaves the door open for negotiation by offering qualified responses like "but we hardly know each other," or "I can't be out late tonight, I have a lot to do tomorrow," he might interpret the message as a "maybe." He may believe that "maybe" he simply needs to get you past your initial objection, and that another drink and a little more persistence just might do the trick. Don't be concerned about coming off as being rude. If he likes you, he'll respect your boundaries and see to it that you get home safely. If he continues his unwanted aggression, make it crystal clear that he is to stop immediately, and leave. If you are at your own place, tell him that your roommate will be home any minute and he needs to go now. If necessary, call campus security or dial 911 for help.

School Shootings

As you are aware, this is an extremely sensitive subject. We all want to protect our children from its known occurrence, but most if not all the solutions posed have become politically charged and hotly debated with little consensus. Earlier in the chapter, you read some startling statistics about the deteriorating mental health of our youth. We already know the brain of a young male doesn't fully mature until his mid-twenties or later, adding to poor and impulsive decisions with little thought about the long-term consequences. Moreover, plenty of respected research points to a strong correlation between bullying and school shootings as well as mental health and school shootings. Then you insert easy access to guns to the mix and well, maybe it all looks like one big, surreal video game to some school shooters. Except, there's no reset button when it ends in the slaughter of our students. I'm not suggesting I have the answer, but I do have an opinion. We should do whatever we can to provide a fear-free learning environment for our kids. Either we need to dramatically step up the availability of quality adolescent mental health care, along with the professional supervision of at-risk youth, or we choke off easy access to guns. At a minimum, restrictions on semi-automatic weapons and related assault-style peripherals (bump stocks, high capacity clips, etc.) would reduce the carnage. Until then, schools can limit points of entry and establish screening checkpoints.

Fortunately, for now, school shootings are still statistically rare and we need to maintain perspective. On average, ten children die each year from school shootings—and, yes, ten too many—yet those are the statistics. Since 1990, there have been 22 shootings at elementary and secondary schools in which two or more people were killed; this tally does not include the shooters who committed suicide. Whereas five of these incidents have occurred over the past five-plus years since 2013, claiming the lives of 27 victims (17 at Parkland), the latter half of the 1990's witnessed seven multiple-fatality shootings with a total of 33 killed (13 at Columbine).

With smartphones for texting and capturing video, active shooter alerts, breaking news coverage and the like, we have exposure to these events like never before. We also have the young, driven survivors of the Parkland shooting and their marches and protests ensuring the issue remains front and center in the public discourse. All of this contributes to a perception that the frequency of the acts has increased markedly. They have not—statistics show they are still uncommon—and that should give no one cause for joy. While gun violence in our schools is less commonplace than gun violence in our society, all of it is pretty sad, and all of it needs to be addressed. In the meantime, if you are a student, teacher, or school staff, there are steps that can be taken to improve your chances of surviving such an ordeal if you are ever faced with it.

Evade

The number one rule is to evade. In other words, immediately determine, if you can, which direction the shots are coming from and run the opposite way, leaving your possessions behind. There is not one material object worth losing your life over. If you are with someone you're responsible for, grab him or her, as well as anyone in your path frozen from fear or shock. But, nonetheless, RUN! at your earliest opportunity and call 911 (this applies for all other options as well).

If Trapped in the Classroom

People don't realize that almost all classroom doors swing out. So, trying to set up a barricade is pointless. You have a better chance running down a hallway than remaining in a classroom awaiting an ambush. Don't hide under a desk and don't cluster together. They used to teach us to hide under a desk in the event of a nuclear blast. That was horrible advice then and it is equally horrible advice in the event of an active shooter. Bullets fired from a 9mm pistol will easily pass through a wooden desk with little deviation and keep going and going. An AR-15 semi-automatic rifle will blast through a cinder block wall. Even more perplexing is that the standard operating procedure for most schools is to huddle students and teacher together in the room, which only makes it that much faster and efficient for a shooter with a semi-automatic weapon to kill dozens of victims and move on to the next classroom of sitting ducks. If you're on a second floor, break windows and jump. Despite the risk of breaking bones, they'll heal. Better yet, have a compact chain or rope ladder in the classroom for emergency escapes. The person outside the classroom with the gun has control. You want to be in control. You don't want to be waiting and hoping if there are any options.

———

If you can't lock the classroom door from the inside, use a sturdy belt and slide the buckle over the door handle. Standing against the adjacent wall, on the side where the door opens, wrap the other end of the belt around your hand and pull the belt tight. This will make it very difficult for the attacker to enter, hopefully encouraging him to move on, and you're safer from gunfire away from the door.

Once the door is secured with the belt, enlist fellow students or a teacher to locate items to use as improvised weapons to engage the shooter should he gain entry. Every classroom has a fire extinguisher. Grab it, pull the pin and discharge the chemical contents in the face of the shooter if he steps across the threshold. If mature and able-bodied, direct a couple of students to position themselves against the wall on both sides of the door. Crouch down low but ready to pounce. Use shirts or bandanas to tie around mouths and noses to keep hands free while providing some breathing protection from the chemical discharge. All other students who cannot hide in a closet or cabinet should spread out and crouch down along the same wall as the door, forcing the shooter to step further into the room to identify targets. This is the moment to engage. Don't hesitate. If you see his head slowly poking through the door to scout out any threats, smash his head with the bottom end of the steel cylinder fire extinguisher or another heavy improvised weapon. If he crosses the threshold or begins firing his weapon, blast him with the extinguisher's chemical contents. Not only will the blast of powdered chemicals obscure the gunman's vision and make it difficult for him to breath (unless he's wearing a gas mask), the unexpected visual disorientation will provide crucial seconds to tackle the weapon first and then the gunman.

If you are hiding in a vulnerable (or opportunistic) spot outside of the classroom as a shooter approaches, circumstances may leave you no other choice but to engage the gunman. If you are within 10 feet or less and have a clear path to either side of or the back of the gunman, do not hesitate. Most school shooters are relatively inexperienced with firearms. Reloading his magazine of ammunition will leave you with at least 5 seconds or more to charge him. If you have an opportunity to tackle the gunman from behind or from the side, go waist high if possible and sling one arm over the weapon to either pull it tight to the gunman or knock it free. Once the gunman has been overpowered, assume he has one or more weapons on him. Don't let him grab for it.

In an active shooter situation, the police may have no idea what is going on upon arrival. Because of this, upon encountering them, raise your hands free of anything in them and immediately obey all their instructions. This is good advice here or in general when encountering the police in an obviously tense situation (and watch and listen closely because any encounter can immediately become tense). The police have a little over a second before they must react to protect themselves, and how many more tragedies do we need to read about where they mistake a cellphone for a weapon? Cops will assume that you are reaching for a weapon. Don't have the phone in your hand to begin with or drop the damn phone before raising your hands. And you don't want to run at a cop, especially if you have something in your hand. Even in an active shooter situation, run to freedom, not at the cops. Again, not only are the police unaware of who the shooters are, but even with your hands raised, you may turn out to be in a line of fire.

These same steps to take are equally applicable for the next section on environmental awareness: workplace violence.

WORKPLACE VIOLENCE

Being at work is another example of a circumstance where you interact with some people you wouldn't necessarily choose to if you weren't getting paid. Unfortunately, violence can be one of the outcomes of a forced co-existence, and it's no longer uncommon at work. Two million people a year are affected by workplace violence, and over 25% of businesses have experienced one violent incident in the past 5 years. Homicide accounted for 500 fatalities in 2016, 10-percent of all fatal workplace injuries.[9] Additionally, an FBI study found that businesses were the setting for nearly half of 160 active-shooter incidents over a 13-year-period. In Gavin De Becker's excellent book *The Gift of Fear*, the author and expert in predicting violence argues that in most instances, we should have seen it coming:

> *"Work place violence is one of the most predictable types of violence because the employee almost always signals his intentions with behaviors common among those who commit such acts at work. Moreover, because it's a work environment, more people are usually around to see these obvious warnings, but, too often, ignore them."*

Workplace violence falls into four categories: criminal intent, customer or client, worker-on-worker, and personal relationship, which overwhelmingly targets women. Disgruntled or terminated employees account for most workplace homicides. Employees who lose their jobs can feel traumatized by the firing with the same emotional impact as the loss of a loved one. Though no employer sets out to deliberately provoke an employee into seeking revenge at the workplace, these homicides often point to business practices that contribute to the violence. De Becker cites three of these company practices in his book:

1. Poor screening and matching of applicants (which leads to knowing very little about who they hire in the first place).
2. Supervisors who bring out the worst characteristics in their employees.
3. The way an employee is fired.

The expression "slow to hire, quick to fire" has merit and should be a general rule. We business owners too often take short cuts in the pre-hiring process because we're eager to fill a position; the candidate (on paper) looks to be suitable, and the candidate didn't make any serious blunders during an in-person interview. Even worse is how slow we are to terminate a problem employee. If a stack of disciplinary write-ups sits in an employee's file and he or she is still working for you, you're asking for trouble of one kind or another. Best practices for safety in the workplace include terminating problem employees the first time they show cause for doing so. Meanwhile, what are some predictive signs that a current employee may turn to a violent act of revenge? Here's a partial list cited by De Becker:[10]

- Blames everyone else for anything that goes wrong and is resistant to change
- Believes someone or everyone is out to get him
- Spends an inordinate amount of time on the computer with activities that have nothing to do with work tasks
- Fascinated with weapons, discusses weapons at work, or owns a weapon
- Often angry, sad, or depressed
- Coworkers fear him
- Has a history of grievances
- Researches or asks questions about workplace security or certain employee's routines
- If fired, maintains contact with current

employees, instead of focusing on finding a new job
- Recent marriage difficulties or relationship problems

If you are concerned about the behaviors of an employee, report it to your supervisor. If your concern isn't taken seriously, take it your supervisor's boss. Any company that is truly committed to safety first for employees will investigate your concerns.

If you are assigned to fire an employee, you probably already know your company's written policies and are familiar with your State's labor laws on terminating workers. But there are other important steps leading up to termination day and during the face-to-face firing that are often overlooked. These steps are especially critical if you are firing an employee who has been a problem or is likely to cause a problem based on past behavior. For starters, confidentiality is essential. If an employee finds out from others he or she is about to be fired, you have provided them with the opportunity to prepare for the outcome and invent reasons why you cannot or should not. Worse, it gives the employee time to prepare for retaliation, potentially using violence.

Rumors of a firing can bring out remarkable and previously unreported issues from an employee who fears that their days at the company are numbered, and most "problem" employees have been to this rodeo before. They are fully aware that, if certain conditions exist, it can legally complicate the termination process and lead to a delay in firing, or even a potentially lucrative lawsuit against their former employer.

The options for bogus claims are numerous, including discrimination, wage and hour theft, retaliation, and wrongful termination. The specific conditions they'll conjure up include a sudden illness or workplace injury, a retaliation claim for being fired after they reported to management inappropriate behavior by another employee or manager ('only to be ignored'), or their filing of a sexual harassment claim ahead of the firing. Maybe you'd be surprised at how many of your employees have worked this scheme at job after job, but I wouldn't be. Working in and around the restaurant, bar, and club scene for years, I've seen it happen dozens of times, leaving the business owners with hefty legal bills and settlements beyond their insurance coverage limits.

If you're a business owner, you probably already know who your problem employees or managers are; they are artful at delivering the bare minimum of the job expected (or less), have excuses on hand at any moment, and deliberately seek out any negative gossip or "dirt" on fellow employees or managers to use as quiet leverage or outright extortion. This doesn't make them homicidal upon termination, but I've never heard of a workplace shooter who was also a model employee.

A terminated employee who feels an overwhelming sense of injustice may look for symbolism in retaliation. Never fire an employee in your office where they may associate the physical place with the devastating news. Let the employee go at the end of the day when fellow workers will be leaving or gone. Fridays are preferable for firing employees, if possible, leaving the weekend to calm down. Immediately shut down access to all company-owned electronics and remove passwords and access codes to security systems and servers. The person tasked to lead the termination should ideally be someone uninvolved with the day-to-day supervision of the employee being fired. This takes personal issues and day-to-day minutia out of the discussion, allowing you to focus only on the documented reasons for ending employment. Make a conscientious effort not to embarrass or humiliate an employee when terminating. Don't engage in any negotiation, and never let the firing be perceived as personal. Always have a witness present, but not a coworker, subordinate, or an intern, as this may humiliate the employee who is being fired. If an employee threatens you or others after you fire them, don't engage with them. Immediately ask security to escort the person off the premises. If there are personal items that need to be retrieved by the terminated employee, be sure to escort and observe them throughout the process.

There's nothing to be gained by putting off the inevitable, but potentially so much to lose. I encourage you to properly prepare and terminate any employee who has shown cause for doing so.

Now that we've examined the various environments where violence may cross your path, and the different challenges each of these environments pose, let's turn now to a different type of awareness—awareness of individuals.

2

AWARENESS OF INDIVIDUALS

Danger usually shows itself. I'm not talking about a natural disaster, a so-called "act of God." I'm talking about the danger posed by another individual. In fact, it is a rarity when danger doesn't show itself...assuming you are paying attention.

Often, it's hard not to see the people who are acting erratically or aggressively. My own experience and statistics show that people looking to perpetrate an assault, especially sexual assault, or to commit some other violent wanton act towards another make their intentions known, or at least send out strong clues, prior to any incident. And danger often shows itself, even with people you know. When it comes to murder specifically, there's at least a 40% chance you'll know your killer, either as a family member or an acquaintance. I'm not suggesting that the clues will always be as clear as a rope, shovel, and bag of lime in your boyfriend's car trunk, but if he does have suspicious stuff stashed, you might want to turn down his invitation to go camping this weekend. And when it comes to sexual assault, the overwhelming majority of victims know the perpetrator, but most are too frightened or embarrassed to report it.

You know from your own experiences that if you think something bad will happen because that is the vibe you're getting, more than likely, you're right. Trust your gut instincts. You've probably processed something internally— consciously or subconsciously—based on the sights, sounds, and even smells of a situation. Suddenly, someone walks in through a door and his or her demeanor causes a red flag to go up. Or you feel uncomfortable because you notice someone acting much more nervous than a situation calls for. Your instincts have heightened your awareness, and that's a good thing.

And as we've seen more and more, this can happen anywhere and at any time. You can feel you're in a completely safe environment or it's a safe time of the day, but unfortunately, potential danger is always around. But I'm not writing this book to scare you. What I hope to do is to have you trusting that you can have a mindset of always looking out while still living your life to the fullest. I'm hoping that you'll become more aware of the people and your surroundings to best minimize the chances that you'll be subject to some sort of violence (or threat of violence) or what to do if, despite this minimization, this same violence or threat becomes real. You want to quickly understand the nature of the threat to determine your best course of action.

So, I've discussed the facts about murder and sexual

assault perpetrated by people you know. But who is it that you don't know that poses your biggest threat?

- **The Hostile-Aggressive Individual**
- **Criminals**

I have broken down our threatening individuals into two main groups—hostile-aggressive individuals and criminals. By "hostile-aggressive individuals," I mean those whose egos are common igniters of violent behavior, and not those who are aggressive in the sense of a competitive athlete or a domineering boss. Often, these aggressive individuals are not the antisocial criminals that I'll soon discuss. These are otherwise normal people who let stress or alcohol get the best of them. These are the "everyday" potential threats that are perhaps the easiest to identify and avoid. These are also the individuals who you're more likely to encounter than the antisocial criminal, but that doesn't mean there's automatically cause for concern.

As an example, I coached high school football for 14 years, and all three of my boys played Little League baseball and AYSO soccer. What I heard and saw from some of the parents over the years was appalling, but most parents were full of hot air and limited their ego-driven outbursts to harsh language, not physical aggression. Case in point, I have several friends named Mike, and one of them is that guy who can't keep his mouth shut at a Little League game. His aggressive language and "passion" for the game (and for his kid playing in the game) is often misunderstood and even misinterpreted as serious threats directed at the opposing team's coach, the umpire, and the volunteer lady on duty at the snack shack! Mike, though standing six-foot four and 220 pounds, isn't violent—he just sounds like a maniac sometimes. He may be obnoxious on occasion, but he's not dangerous, and if you ask him to sit down and be quiet, he complies...for an inning or two, at least! Other aggressive individuals, though, may not be as harmless as Mike and that's the truly hostile-aggressive person you need to recognize, avoid, or confront with caution.

The Hostile-Aggressive Individual

Most of us have seen it first-hand, or heard about it once or more: someone who crosses the line from being the fan, the father, teacher, firefighter, or corporate executive, to being the violent aggressor. Pent up stress, money problems, relationship issues, or pressures at the office are just some of many things that may be going on underneath the surface of an otherwise *typical* guy that can ignite a violent fuse if provoked, especially if he's been drinking. If a hostile-aggressive guy is acting rudely, jabbing your index finger into his chest and lecturing him on manners won't get him to sit down and shut up. Just the opposite, it's like pushing the plunger on a demolition-sized bundle of dynamite.

So how do you tell the difference between a harmless blowhard and someone who may snap with brutal consequences? That's the problem. Unless you know them personally, you can't. What you can do though is control your own words and actions to avoid provoking a hostile-aggressive person and giving them an excuse to overreact.

My experience has shown me that what usually triggers violent, hostile-aggressive behavior is the perception held by the aggressor that somehow you've disrespected them (or their space, people, religion, race, team, etc.), and in their minds, they have the right and the duty to aggressively respond, if for no other reason than to "teach you a lesson." Whatever spontaneous flash of rudeness you may have perpetrated, perhaps without being aware of your own thoughtless actions, the potentially volatile situation can almost always be quickly defused with a few words: "Sorry, my apologies, no disrespect intended."

With 810,000 incidents of aggravated assault in 2017 (65% of all violent crimes in the U.S.), we'll never know how much physical pain, emergency room bills, arrests for battery, criminal and civil legal claims, and attorney's fees may have been prevented with a simple, momentary ego check and an apology. People need and deserve to be respected.

The more dangerous hostile-aggressive individuals may suffer from pathological anger, an especially severe diagnosis of post-traumatic stress disorder (PTSD), or have had a recent crisis in their life. Drugs or alcohol can act to either bruise an ego that perhaps would not have been bruised otherwise, or make an already bad situation worse. As I mentioned in the previous chapter, one of your best chances of being involved in a violent situation is with someone who's drunk. With their filters and rationality lowered, they often act or react in a completely different way than if they were sober. If you've been drinking too, you're likely to do the same.

However, there are other warning signs exhibited by

hostile-aggressive individuals which aren't necessarily directly linked to alcohol or drug use:

- Social withdrawal and isolation
- Quick loss of temper
- Expressions of violence (verbal or illustrated)
- Intolerance to others who aren't like them

If you're confronted by a hostile-aggressive individual who exhibits irrational anger, along with any of the other behaviors listed above, the best course of action is to avoid them! If you know them from school or work, don't engage them without professional help. With hostile-aggressive people, the confrontation typically occurs because the person who does decide to engage cannot control their own ego or emotions. In this instance, you need to be aware of your own self—the changes in your own behavior when challenged—to avoid conflict. If you can't avoid the individual, keep your distance (at least six feet away to give you time to act or react). Keep your cool and don't escalate the situation. The aggressor may try to push your hot buttons, but don't take the bait. Be assertive but diplomatic in your words in your attempt to stop the aggressive behavior, and then leave if possible.

While there are endless examples of ego-driven and hostile-aggressive behavior, I want to focus on two areas in particular because of their frequency and relevancy:

- **Violence on the road**
- **Bullying at school**

Violence on the Road

Most ego-driven violence on our roadways can be attributed to road rage, followed by violence occurring because of car accidents. By the time you reach my age, we all have road rage stories, mostly from our youth, either from personal experience or from our buddies. Some of the stories, where no one was injured, are even humorous in hindsight. There's my friend Bryan, and his friend Deken, who stopped to scold a group of teenagers who had darted across a six-lane highway at night and forced Deken to aggressively brake and swerve to avoid hitting them. Deken rolled down his window to deliver a brief (and sarcastic) safety lecture and was rewarded with a warm carton of chicken chow mein, beautifully side-armed by one of the high school boys, through the open window of his 1985 Oldsmobile Cutlass. The direct hit to Deken's chest allowed the syrupy contents of the carton to explode onto his face and up to the interior roof of his car. His initial reaction (after wiping the noodles and sauce from his eyes) was to verbally threaten to kill the kid who threw the chow mein. Before he could exit the car, he was immediately hit again with a side of steamed rice! These were high school kids, so what could they do but laugh?

Then there's Tim, who swapped trucks with his boss one day, cut off another driver, pulled up to the traffic light next to him, and watched in horror as the guy who was cut off (an off-duty fireman) pulled an axe from his trunk and buried into the side of his boss' Dodge Durango. The axe lodged so deeply that the fireman couldn't pull it out. Gabe, a passenger in the back, and who ironically sports a tattoo on his chest spelling out *"Anger is a Gift,"* narrowly escaped out the opposite door after first fumbling with the child locks. The fireman fled to his car and sped away, perhaps forgetting that the county-issued fire axe had his station number and address stamped on the handle. Certain decisions can't be undone. The road-rager is now formerly a fireman, and 15 years later, Gabe still defends his chest tattoo to his wife whenever his kid is throwing a tantrum.

Here's one last road rage story that's more recent and sums up the randomness of road rage encounters. Roughly a year ago, my brother-in-law Rodney was driving to a farmers' market with my sister and Rodney's sister, near Colorado Springs where they live. The drive to the market is only a few miles away and it was a beautiful Sunday morning. He was traveling 65 mph, the speed limit, when a truck came up on his rear bumper, tailgating at first, and then blaring his horn. Rodney was about to move a lane over when this guy passed on the left using the turning lane. As he passed, he moved his right arm in a violent stabbing motion, then slowed down in front of Rodney, trying to provoke an altercation.

Rodney was understandably fuming, but with his wife and sister in the car, he waived off his initial plan to stop and confront the hostile driver. In the news the next day, the same guy was arrested for attacking multiple people at a nearby park with a hatchet, and had murdered another hiker at a trail next to the park. Police in Woodland Park, Colorado found out that this guy had also murdered two female hikers in Kansas just days earlier. The road-rager with the toma-hawk air chop to Rodney was a killer on a spree...good thing my brother-in-law chose to ignore him!

With serious road rage, when you cut someone off and they're screaming at you, quite often their ego has immediately taken them to a place where they think you were deliberately trying to kill them. If you did accidentally cut them off, acknowledge your mistake with a friendly hand in the air, as if it to say, "I'm guilty, sorry." If they persist in dogging you, doing things such as exiting the highway or ignoring this person are ways to deal with or defuse this mindset. Pulling over to confront the other driver face to face is a huge mistake. Remember, one of my golden rules of self-defense is to always assume the other person is carrying a weapon. Are you really prepared to confront someone who pulls out a knife, handgun, or an axe or hatchet? For what...?

————

And by the way, as a preventative measure, if you're going to cut someone off, make sure their car isn't covered with bumper stickers. A recent study found that drivers who display bumper stickers (a motorist's form of territorial markers) were significantly more likely to exhibit signs of road rage.[11] The more stickers on the car, the greater the chance of the driver becoming unglued if you invade their space. The study further concluded that the tone of the bumper sticker messages made no difference in the increase of road rage incidents, only the quantity of stickers on the car. I guess the lesson here is whether a driver's bumper sticker reads "I Flunked Anger Management Class" or "I Brake for Butterflies," isn't by itself a clue to how the driver may respond to your obnoxious tailgating. However, if multiple messages are slapped across the back of the vehicle in front of you, it may be best to slow down, change lanes, or pull off the highway for a cheeseburger!

Fights over parking spaces are another common form of road rage. If an angry driver stops and leaps out of his car in a parking lot (believing you had taken a parking spot he was waiting for) and heads directly toward you as you exit your car, you better be ready to defend yourself. This guy believes a huge injustice has just occurred, probably on top of a lot of other perceived injustices and recent personal issues. You may end up the target of his frustration. Warn the potential attacker to stay back, but if he continues toward you (into your attack zone), strike first, using only sufficient force to stop the hostile action. Of course, if you really did jack his parking spot, man up and apologize.

Car accidents generate the second-most incidents of ego-driven violence. If you're involved in a traffic accident, the law requires you to pull over and exchange information. But first, call 911 (or have a witness or someone else call 911 if you're unable). If the other driver is overly agitated or threatening in any way, return to your car, lock your doors, and wait for assistance to arrive before dealing with this individual. If you think this sounds like common sense, this is what an off-duty sheriff's deputy failed to do recently in San Bernardino, California. The other driver, a convicted felon, exited his vehicle and delivered a single fatal punch to the officer's head.

The point is that since accidents can and do bring out

hostile behavior in people, if you're in an accident, alert the police first, and never assume the other person involved is understanding, or even decent, like you. They probably are, but use caution anyhow.

Bullying at School

Being bullied is feeling powerless. I recently read a blog post about bullying written by an adult reflecting on his childhood. He wrote, "Being a victim of bullying means not fighting back, for fear that you'll be hit even harder. It means following the school's rules about fighting, which means being obligated to simply endure as much abuse as the bullies can generate."

Sadly, his statement rings equally true today. Roughly one in five students is bullied, and one-third of these middle and high school kids are being bullied once or twice a month during the school year. And while the school authorities attempt to sort things out, what is it teaching these significant number of bullied students? It teaches them to accept the verbal and physical assaults and to languish in fear for months (or more). It teaches victims—incorrectly—that they are powerless to stop the attacks in the interim. And even worse, it teaches victims that it's okay to be victimized. It teaches acceptance, which only perpetuates the problem.

Bullying is about communicating social hierarchy. A recent study of middle and high school students by the University of California at Davis showed that the more popular a kid becomes, the more central they are to the school's social network, and the more aggressive their behavior becomes, including bullying.[12] The old notion that schoolyard bullies were from unhappy homes, friendless, or otherwise inadequate turns out to be wrong. Bullies are often popular and smart, though the most popular 5% of students in the study didn't bully. Neither did the kids at the very bottom of the popularity food chain. They don't need to. Bullying is a form of social combat which influences a student's status in the hierarchy of popularity. The students at the top of the social hierarchy are the most popular and have nothing to gain by bullying others, but have more to lose. Those at the bottom lack the capacity to bully and simply wait for someone above them to be knocked down in status by another student and then try and step into the vacancy. As to why some students in the middle of the spectrum choose to bully others, the main reason seems to be that aggressive behavior toward another student makes it clear in front of others that, in their mind, they outrank that individual socially. The more they assert their rank, the higher their perceived popularity.[13]

So, your response to a bully must reflect the facts that this is not true, and that it is of no consequence. In other words, if you're the one being bullied, you must relay that you don't believe the bully has a higher status than you and that you don't care what they think of you.

If a bully attempts to demean you (e.g. regarding your acne, like "hey crater-face"), don't ignore it or reply in anger. Both responses reveal that you do care what they think of you, and thus that they outrank you. Instead, respond with something that suggests that you outrank them (e.g. "keep talking, I'm diagnosing your impairment...") or something that suggests that you consider their statement to have been made in jest (e.g. "thank you for all the attention you've been giving to my beautiful face…"). Yes, humor can be a survival skill. Many comedians report that they were bullied when they were younger and developed a quick wit as their defense, which proved successful.

That said, what you say isn't as important as how you say it. Self-esteem works wonders against bullying. When you respond, you need to smile, lean back, and laugh a little. You need to communicate the fact that you are the higher status person and they are the weaker person with something to prove.

If a bully wants to fight and fights better than you, then you better know how to fight back. Otherwise, you may just provide them with the opportunity to show that they're stronger than you and further enhance their status. Learning to box or training in a street-smart martial art (discussed later) is helpful, even if you don't end up fighting. Just the fact that you know how to fight will give you a more confident, calmer body language, making it less likely that you'll be bullied to begin with or that a bully will continue with their aggression toward you. Why pick on you—a potential challenge (making you a more difficult target) and a challenge they may lose (an unthinkable outcome)—when there are easier victims around?

If a bully insists on fighting and you're not ready to defend yourself, don't accept their time frame. Quietly backing down or fighting them in this instance feeds right into their assertion of dominance. Don't take the bait. Instead, say something that suggests that you don't believe fighting is an intelligent solution, such as "Yeah, I hear you fight a lot." Shake your head in utter disdain and walk away.

Sometimes you do need to engage in a little violence, but never escalate it beyond the level that they deserve given their behavior towards you. Bullies hate pain (and losing status) as much anyone, and delivering a dose of it usually stops the bullying without causing serious injury to anyone.

If you do decide to physically engage with the bully, though, and this happens in a school environment, you may end up facing disciplinary consequences, as will be discussed in the *Law of Self-Defense* chapter. It is ludicrous that victims of bullying are punished by schools, regardless of the underlying facts, and thankfully the idea of "zero toler-ance" when it comes to using self-defense in schools is changing somewhat, but not fast enough. Despite the possi-bility of school punishment, you may still feel it's worth the price if it stops you from being bullied further.

If you witness bullying, nothing says "high status" quite like sticking up for other people. More than half of bullying situations (57%) stop when a peer intervenes on behalf of the student being bullied. If a bully is bullying you, then chances are they're bullying someone else too. If you see a bully picking on someone, confront him and calmly point out that his behavior is out of line. It's the right thing to do, and it's a clear assertion of authority. The more popular you are in your school, the more powerful your intervening will be in sending the message that bullying isn't the path to becoming the prom king.

Bullying is also a way that people assert their member-ship in, or gain access to, a group. If you're an outsider—of a different race, intelligence level, from a perceived lower household net worth, or sexual orientation not understood or respected by others—you're likely to get bullied simply because you're the outsider. How do you fight a group? In this case, the best solution is just to be proud of your difference; go find people, outside of your school environment if necessary, that will not only identify with you, but also welcome and appreciate your friendship.

Criminals

Let's move on to the second and more dangerous of our two groups—the true criminal. These individuals are almost always characterized by their antisocial behavior, which has been shown to be the number one attribute related to violent crime. These are the individuals who steal, mug, rape, and murder. Some will commit an assault because they are bored —an attack gives them the intense excitement they desire and provides the rush they feel they need—others kill out of anger, physiological fear, or because the victim doesn't practice their same religious or political doctrine. Regardless, all of this is abnormal, truly antisocial behavior.

While the inebriated are the easiest to avoid, the antisocial criminal who has specifically targeted an individual is the hardest.

Criminals believe that they have a right to perpetrate these violent acts. And while all have antisocial behavior and exhibit symptoms of antisocial personality disorder (ASPD), degrees of such behavior and the severity of such disorder exist. Sociopaths represent the most egregious, harmful, or dangerous behavior patterns of those with ASPD. Full antisocial sociopaths—the serial killers and rapists—have no empathy whatsoever and, fortunately, are somewhat rare. Most criminals are not sociopaths, but blame others for their plight. They have a deep sense of disillusionment and anger issues. They feel as if society has wronged them in some way or another, and their mindset is one of you owing them the contents of your car or house or the gold chain around your neck because of it.

Most criminals are cocky and don't believe that anyone will ever try to stop them or that they'll get caught. Part of this mentality comes from the fact that criminals typically choose vulnerable targets. While the news may label a crime as "senseless," what the criminals are doing makes sense to them; their behavior is both premeditated and deliberate. This doesn't mean that, in most instances, their actions aren't hasty, but they have typically scoped out their victim, albeit for only a few seconds perhaps, in advance before acting.

The criminal's true belief is that they will prevail in their illegal endeavors, especially by preying on the vulnerable—who not only deserve what is coming to them, but who criminals feel cannot or will not fight back. This criminal behavior enhances their sense of power and control, resulting in a trail of carnage.

How can you be on the lookout for these bad guys? In many cases, these individuals will stand out; you just need to be aware. Individual awareness is establishing a baseline for what is typical and expected behavior, dress, or demeanor for the environment. By observing an anomaly, you can look for further clues that signal trouble. No single anomaly is usually enough information to act, but several combined require immediate action.

A good number of criminals will stare at their intended victim prior to acting. Most criminals think they're smart, but they're not, and staring at someone they're about to do something to is not the brightest of ideas. It can and should alert an intended victim to potential trouble if they're paying enough attention to the people around them.

It's not uncommon for criminals or terrorists to carry their weapons in bags or backpacks, and while many people nowadays carry backpacks, if the backpack is out of place or the individual carrying the backpack is throwing off bad vibes, trust your instincts. A suspicious cop stopped a man with a large duffel bag who was acting strangely and had gotten off the light rail outside of Pasadena, California. It turns out there were three AR-15s in the bag and the man was on his way to a school. The cop sensed that there was no reason for that man to have a duffel bag of that size. In 1988, while I was attending San Gabriel High School, I passed a fellow student in the hall carrying a similar bag. It struck me as odd, but we simply chatted a few words in passing. Soon thereafter, the student, Jeff Cox, was holding a classroom hostage with the rifle he had pulled from the bag. My instincts were the same as the cop's, yet at that time, my actions were different. I now know better. Cox was released from prison in 1993, and subsequently murdered and dismembered a man in Phoenix, stuffing him in a huge icebox at a storage facility hundreds of miles away in Van Nuys, California. He was arrested by the FBI and convicted and sent back to prison after a two-day power failure in the neighborhood led to a ghastly odor wafting from the storage unit.

So, look for things that appear out of place. Does the day call for someone to be wearing such a large overcoat? Look for the out-of-place vehicle. Look for the out-of-place individual. Look for the potential malcontent based on their appearance or demeanor. I'm not saying that a guy with facial or neck tattoos, or driving a low rider car with the music blaring, or wearing a hoodie or baggy pants with lots of bling, is necessarily bad news, because you can't judge a book by its cover. Although, I do think your cautionary defenses should be up.

———

I remember looking out the window one afternoon in my 6th grade class only to spot Ralph, our pet wolf, wandering into the school's outdoor lunch area, sending dozens of third-graders fleeing in panic. At 160 pounds, Ralph was bigger than your average pet, and admittedly looked a bit menacing when hungry. But he was, in fact, the sweetest four-legged friend I had ever known. To these surprised 8-year-olds however, Ralph was proof that either they had been lied to or that the villain in the story of *The Three Little Pigs* had been misclassified as fictional. They screamed and scrambled while Ralph moonwalked on the tables, devouring the abandoned booty of corn dogs, fruit cups, and peanut butter squares. Michael Jackson's *Thriller* album had just been released, and Ralph's theme song was clearly "Don't Stop 'Til You Get Enough."

Ralph the wolf was harmless. He just looked different, and that was enough to scare people. The same could be said for Sonny Hughes, a mentor of mine who opened my eyes to exploring the benefits of other disciplines outside of Shotokan, who taught me Judo and Muay Thai, and who definitively proved to me that you can't judge people just by what you initially see. To me, a high school kid, Sonny was an extremely scary guy; he was a colorful character, and an insanely intense sensei who believed that you had to experience physical pain to properly dish it out. Being younger and athletic, I was drawn to his aggressive style, especially the creative ways he would effortlessly deliver pain to precise points on the head and body that I never knew could cause such agony. Yet, he was a contradiction on so many fronts. Sonny, a guy with four tenth-degree black belts and who could swiftly beat the crap out of you, was, by day, a hairdresser to the stars! Yes, his hands could be lethal...or they could just as easily lather in shampoo and gently massage scalps. I eventually learned he'd been raised by the famous actor Mickey Rooney and Rooney's second wife, B.J. Baker, a renowned singer. He was a stunt man in dozens of movies, hung out with Elvis Presley for years (teaching him judo and jiu-jitsu in between concerts and recording sessions), and was even a guest of Johnny Carson on *The Tonight Show* in the early 1970's. The "scariest" person I had ever met, it turned out, was also creative, entertaining, and worked a blow dryer like Vidal Sassoon!

Like I said, don't judge a book by its cover. But that's not to say that you shouldn't be more alert if your intuition is telling you to pay closer attention to an individual. Look for red flags. These days they can be subtle. For example, someone unknown to you and covered in tattoos used to be an almost automatic signal to proceed with caution. But are people with tattoos still reason enough for us to be extra cautious? After all, four out of ten U.S. adults aged 18 to 69 now have at least one tattoo.[14] Two decades ago, there was an association between tattoos and alcohol, drug use, violence, sexual activity, eating disorders, and even suicide. But that's not the case anymore. If anything, people with tattoos and piercings are perceived by some as being more rebellious than people without tattoos, but most people now don't perceive any difference.

Hold on though. Apparently, something does happen when people go heavy on the ink (four or more tattoos or piercings). A 2010 study of body art and its connection to deviance found that those who push the envelope with tattoos and piercings have a high need for sensation and are far more likely to participate in risky or deviant behaviors. While the study found no connection to higher levels of deviance among the participants who sported one or two tats, it found that heavily tatted people were ten times more likely to have an arrest history, a four-fold increase in drug use other than marijuana, and a five-fold increase in having had nine or more sex partners in the last year.[15] And, for what it's worth, several studies have also shown that those diagnosed with Psychopathic or Sadistic personalities, or with Borderline or Antisocial Personality Disorders, were more likely to be tattooed than not.

Inmates and ex-cons are also more likely to be tattooed, many of them getting inked while serving time. There are several reasons why. In an environment like a prison, where there are limited opportunities for self-expression, tattoos can often convey gang or group membership, devotion to a person or cause, past incarceration, or promote individuality. Regardless, there's no clear evidence that a couple of tattoos point to criminality. Nevertheless, if you run across an individual with tattoos covering their entire neck, head, and face, I'm certain you'll spot their uniqueness, maybe even admire their self-expression, but I am also advising you to raise your overall awareness level within the context of your environment. Are you at a dog park where your French Bulldog is sharing a ball with Mr. Body Art's Doberman named *Sugar*, or is he loitering alone outside the door of a 24-hour convenience store at midnight? Context matters.

Since tattoos aren't a singularly reliable sign of criminal intent, we need to be aware of other signals which may indicate looming trouble. Generalization or not, criminals tend to walk with a swagger. Again, it's their ill-placed sense of invulnerability, and it's also a potential heads-up to us. But one thing's for sure, irrespective of factors like race, age, color, or religion, people share common physical responses, conscious and subconscious, to certain stressful situations in the same way. Criminals and terrorists are no different, and the commission of a crime or an act of terror is a stressful situation, even for the perpetrator. So, in these situations, bad guys almost always tip their hand before they attack. What are some stress signals you can look for?

- Frequent, subconscious patting or tapping something under their coat, shirt, or pants pocket or waistband (brings assurance to the criminal that the weapon or explosive is still in place)
- Body language (guarded, arms crossed, staring)
- Dilated pupils/rapid blinking
- Faster breathing
- Flushed face or paling
- Dry mouth
- Sweaty palms
- Trembling
- Anxious/nervous behavior
- Frequently checking to see if anyone is following them
- Smells and acts like he's been drinking (alcohol is a factor in 40% of all violent crimes)

Predatory criminals, on the other hand, are opportunistic, targeting their victims when and where they choose, and because they are certain they will quickly overwhelm them, they are confident of escaping unharmed with whatever possessions they were seeking. They will strike fast and furious, often after luring you close enough to them to leave no space or time for you to react, even if you are trained to defend yourself. You can throw out most behavioral observations above because the predator will be upon you before you know it. They'll be overly nice, pretending to be needing something as simple as the time of day, or by offering their assistance to you if you appear lost or struggling with packages. They unleash their violence as soon as they're close enough to guarantee themselves a strike you'll never see coming and can't defend.

Nevertheless, these predatory criminals still show themselves before striking, albeit quickly. They engaged your attention under a false pretense to get close to you without raising suspicion, and you (being the kind person you are) didn't want to appear unfriendly or unhelpful. You inadvertently broke the cardinal rule of *Inside-Out Self-Protection*: never let a potential threat into your attack zone! So, does that mean you need be aloof to every stranger that approaches you? It depends. Are you a tourist, or are you on your own familiar turf? Is the stranger a little old lady or an able-bodied man or woman? Are you alone, are your hands full, were you approached in the open space of an active neighborhood park or in an area limiting your escape and visibility by others (parked cars, stairwell, elevator)? Without even consciously processing the variables in the moment, your intuition will alert you if something doesn't feel right. Listen to it.

One of the hardest things for good people to do is to be cynical and seem cold and callous to someone who looks friendly enough and asks nicely for a moment of their time. If you live in a big city, it's depressing to think that you need be so guarded, so jaded, and so ready for exploitation that humanity is no longer an option when dealing with strangers. Like I said before, it depends on the circumstances. People living in small towns aren't immune either. In August of 2018, Mollie Tibbetts, 20, was jogging along a rural road outside of Brooklyn, Iowa (population 1,400) when a 24-year-old man with no criminal record parked his car and started running alongside her. Mollie grabbed her phone and threatened to call the police. The man panicked, kidnapped and killed her, and buried her body in a secluded area of a cornfield. The young man might have acted very friendly to Mollie Tibbetts in his unusual approach to meet her, but she knew something wasn't right, and unfortunately, she only threatened to call the police instead of immediately dialing 911 (which minimally would have signaled her location via GPS).

In this horrible crime, the murderer showed himself before attacking. Surveillance video from nearby businesses shows him driving past the victim several times before stopping his car and inviting himself to join her on her jog. Mollie apparently didn't notice this, even on a remote two-lane road. Like many of us, she was wearing ear buds and was probably enjoying the solitude of her run, perhaps escaping the stress of college for a moment. The predator showed himself a second time when he approached Mollie, suddenly jogging alongside her. Let me repeat that. *She was jogging alone on a rural highway when approached by a stranger who decided himself to join her.* I think that qualifies as an anomaly, certainly unusual behavior, and out of context for the environment. It didn't matter that perhaps the uninvited man didn't look or act intimidating at first. He had already raised several red flags! Let's learn from Mollie's tragedy; small town or big city, overly friendly people should be viewed with an eye toward extreme caution, and if you're alarmed enough to threaten someone with calling the police, just call the police first! You can always cancel the 911 call for assistance if the threat goes away.

Overly friendly and overly helpful people should raise your awareness level just as much as the unengaged stranger who exhibits dress or behaviors that are odd for the environment or situation. Again, if your gut feeling tells you something isn't right, even in the presence of a very friendly stranger, don't ignore it. An overly friendly person either wants to sell something you probably don't want or intends to do you harm. My apologies to all of you in sales, I understand you're just doing your job. A professionally trained salesperson understands that it's not productive or good for their brand to invade your personal space or keep pressing after a couple of reasonable attempts to overcome your objections, and an *unprofessional* salesperson isn't selling anything worth buying. Similarly, an overly friendly or overly helpful person should be engaged with caution. There are no absolutes in the mental sorting bins where we separate kind acts of strangers from manipulative maneuvers and dangerous people, but my general rule of thumb is to be wary of help from strangers who select you to be the beneficiary of their benevolence. In general,

- **friendly people** offer their assistance when asked.
- **overly friendly people** offer their assistance without being asked and won't take "no" for an answer.

The nice man who approaches you to offer help carrying your groceries into your apartment should be smart enough to understand that his act of kindness requires you to take an unnecessary risk with a stranger. If he won't take no for an answer, put the groceries down and call the police.

Look, I'm not saying you should live in a bubble or live in fear. But I always take stock of what's around me, and that is my advice to you. Just open your eyes and be aware. It's rare that a criminal or predator isn't giving off some signal or another. If you feel uncomfortable, you're probably not wrong. But too often, people don't trust their intuition. They deny their gut instincts and rationalize it as paranoia. But if you're observing several of the telltale signs of trouble discussed above (and the context of the person's behavior is not reasonable), you are far better off taking appropriate action than remaining quiet. Not all violence is the same, and you'll choose your best course of action if you can identify who you are dealing with, although the best course of action will almost always be to get away or get out if you can.

When I say not all violence is the same, I'm mainly speaking of the difference between a typical bar fight or a mugging, for example, compared with a serious fight for your life, where the person or persons you're dealing with could care less about the value of your life or any human life. These are vicious people, and many will kill you without batting an eye. There is no comparison between getting into an altercation with these types of criminal monsters and sociopaths, and the guy at a friend's wedding who insulted you in front of your girlfriend. Altercations with these violent people can escalate quickly and become out of control. When you see it, you'll know it, and this is no time to let your ego get the best of you, as I did years ago. Let me provide you with a cautionary tale to stress my point.

In the spring of 1986, I was involved in a violent fight that would shape the way I look at myself and the way I would react to any altercation from that day forward. I was with my good buddy Brian, casually driving to the Trader Joe's market on Arroyo Parkway in Pasadena. We were traveling south on Marengo Avenue when, at a stoplight, we saw an elderly woman crossing the street very slowly. She was handicapped and fragile. Suddenly, an older beat-up Camaro stopped next to us, music blaring, and the driver started shouting at the elderly woman, spewing out vulgar words and names. Brian shouted at them to knock it off and they shouted back at us. At the time, we could only see two people in the front seat, and Brian looked at me with intense eyes and asked if I wanted to "kick some f*@king ass." The Camaro turned into the alley behind the market and we followed. Brian leaped out of the car, barely putting the gear into "park." Seconds later, Brian was pulling the driver out of the car by his hair, head-butting him while dragging him into the alley. The other man emerged from the passenger side of the car, walking toward me while removing his shirt, exposing his chest and neck covered with tattoos. The dense markings continued uninterrupted up his neck and covered his face.

When he was within about 10 feet, I intercepted him by taking a big left step straight at him, launching a punch directly at his mouth. I felt my fist drive through his face and he snapped and fell backwards, violently hitting his head on the ground and knocking him unconscious.

Much to my surprise, a third individual leaped from the back seat of the Camaro and began furiously kicking Brian in the head as he was rolling around on the ground with the driver. I lunged at the kicking man, my forearm landing across his chest, slamming him into a cinder block wall 15 feet behind him. He collapsed, screaming in pain. As I turned my attention to the guy rolling around on the asphalt with Brian, a fourth man appeared and pointed a .45 semi-automatic pistol at my head and announced he was going to kill me! For whatever reason—instinct, loyalty, or stupidity—I ignored the guy with the gun, made my way over to my buddy, and threw the attacker off. Brian was now bleeding profusely and semi-conscious.

The guy that I had knocked out earlier with a single punch was now on his feet and staggering towards the Camaro, blood pouring from his mouth and nose, and yelling at his buddies to get in their car and leave. The gunman was helping the derelict that I had slammed into the brick wall back into the Camaro. Brian was in bad shape with a broken nose, head lacerations, and bleeding eyes. I drove us back to my house where my dad treated his wounds. It was at that point that we realized both of our wallets were gone and that these dudes we had just fought now knew where we lived.

Fortunately, the guys in the Camaro were pulled over by the San Gabriel Police, who searched the injured and bloody occupants and found our wallets. Many on the San Gabriel Police force were my father's patients and they recognized my driver's license. At the police station later that day, we were informed that three of the guys we fought had just been released from state prison. They had been taken to a local hospital for their injuries. One man, the guy I slammed into the wall, apparently had broken his back from the impact.

I don't know why I wasn't shot that day. We should have paid no attention to those guys and just ensured that the elderly woman made it safely across the street and driven off. Had I been alert and aware, all the signs were there that these were sociopaths who had no value for life or empathy. I am beyond lucky that I was not dead at age 16.

3

SELF-AWARENESS

"We have met the enemy and he is us."
- Walt Kelley

Self-awareness in self-defense is important for several reasons. First, the way you carry yourself may unwittingly provide easy opportunities for predators and criminals to strike, making you a "soft" target. Additionally, you may be surprised to learn that your choice of friends and the activities you choose to engage in are strongly linked to your chances of being victimized by violent crime. Finally, it's especially helpful to be aware of and to understand how your own body's built-in physiological response to a serious threat works, and how too often, it can work against you.

Many people freeze in the face of danger, like a deer caught in the headlights of car, or a thief in the night that freezes when a light is shined on him. As humans, like most mammals, we instinctively stop movement to avoid drawing the attention of a threatening animal or person. Unfortunately, freezing up is the worst thing you can do when facing a violent encounter. Knowledge and training can help prevent the paralysis of sudden freezing from happening, replacing it instead with action. If that unthinkable moment happens to you, and your life is in jeopardy, you have three options: run, hide, or fight. Wasting precious time thinking about your options may cost you your life. Doing nothing and freezing in place will almost certainly end poorly. I'll go into much greater detail on this subject when I discuss the *Outside* portion of my training because regardless of how we react, that reaction is physical in nature, even if we freeze in place. So, the real focus of this chapter is to make you aware of certain characteristics of self that relate to victimization. A good understanding of these characteristics (followed by an honest, critical self-analysis) may bring to the surface any necessary changes you may need to make regarding your own habits, demeanor, friends, and activities, and will go a long way to ensuring as best you can that violence does not find you, or vice versa, that you do not find violence.

BECOME A HARD TARGET

As the last chapter pointed out, criminals prefer to target those who are the most vulnerable. Criminals often perceive women and seniors as weaker, slower, and unable or unwilling to defend themselves. Experienced criminals make their assessment of their next potential target in a matter of a few seconds. Does he or she look distracted, lost, meek, or nervous? They may not be the brightest people, but they know that picking out a potential victim who (by all appearances) looks like he or she won't fight back, won't cause a scene, will instantly comply, and doesn't look like they can fight back is an easy, "soft" target. The antidote, of course, is to make you a perceived "hard" target.

Let's start with your own posture and overall demeanor and dress. Do you walk with poise and purpose, with your shoulders back and chin up slightly? All of this makes you appear taller and, more importantly, confident. Do you make very brief eye contact with passersby (just to let them know you are aware of them) or scan your head from side to side as you walk, looking behind you routinely as well? Do you look keenly attentive to the things and people around you? If the answer is "yes," then you've made yourself a harder target. What you choose to wear isn't a factor. Even for sexual predators, statistics show that what a victim is wearing has nothing to do with their being targeted. It's *how you carry yourself* and your perceived ability and willingness to fight back.

Let's take it one step further. Do you walk with one or more persons, especially at night? If alone, do you stick to well-lit, well-travelled streets in familiar neighborhoods? Criminals and predators look for opportunities to strike that are optimal for them to succeed unharmed and undetected. Avoid isolated areas. Well-lit places with people around provide much less opportunity for successful strikes. If you take away easy opportunities, you've made yourself an even harder target.

A vulnerable person, or soft target, on the other hand, is someone who looks nervous. They often take strides that are rt or too long when walking, or walk hunched over ..·.ın their heads down. In the process, they are non-verbally communicating to anyone paying attention that they are clueless of their surroundings. Similarly, don't appear oblivious. If your eyes are cast down and checking the latest text message on your smartphone, and your ear buds are installed to wash away the sounds of life around you, you have made yourself an easier target.

A better use of your smartphone may be one of several safety apps you can download. Noonlight© is a mobile application that can be downloaded by anyone for personal safety and security reasons. If you're walking to school or into a parking garage, for example, just open the app and have it ready. If you sense a feeling of being unsafe, keep a finger on the screen's "hold until safe" button. Removing your finger triggers a screen asking for a four-digit pin. If you enter the code, that's your signal to dispatchers that you're safe. If you don't, Noonlight© calls the police and uses GPS to send them to your location.

Another fast-growing app is offered by Titan HST and helps communication during an emergency. Schools use it to better communicate to students and parents during fires, floods, or earthquakes, but it can also be used in the event of a school lockdown or shooting. It can more precisely locate students (even if they're hiding) and deliver up-to-the-minute information to students, teachers, and parents. Businesses are also using the app as part of their emergency preparedness and response planning.

THE IMPACT OF FRIENDS AND ACTIVITIES

Avoiding a violent attack by making yourself a hard target or never giving criminals an easy opportunity to strike lowers the odds of your being victimized. But are the odds stacked against you if you're a minority and live in a lower income neighborhood? Is violence likely to find you no matter what you do? My house on Roses Road in the city of San Gabriel was only three blocks south of the wealthy suburb of San Marino and across the street from San Gabriel Country Club, a 100-year-old private golf club which admitted only white members until the early 1990's. Across the street from the clubhouse was my dad's doctor's office on Las Tunas Drive, and just a quarter mile to the south was Broadway Avenue, which was the border of the Sangra gang neighborhood.

Later, San Gabriel also became home to the new Asian street gangs known as the "Asian Boyz" and the international street gang known as "Wah Ching." These Asian gangs became more prevalent in the late 1980's and early 1990's and attributed to, among other things, a brutal double murder on Lombardy Place in San Marino, only a half-mile north of my house. But here I was, an upper-class white kid living in a beautiful house by the Country Club, just a few blocks from a completely different world. As I walked to my friends' houses in the rougher neighborhoods, I would pass walls with graffiti reading "Sangra Rifa." "Sangra" means "blood" and "Rifa" translates into "the baddest." Further into other neighborhoods were the spray-painted traffic signs and building walls covered with different graffiti, the territorial markers for Lomas, who were the bigger and older gang from

South San Gabriel, Rosemead, Whittier Narrows, and parts of Montebello. There were huge fights or rumbles between Sangra and Lomas, and my brother Robbie witnessed his close friend being murdered with a shotgun that had suddenly emerged from a low rider's car window. The blast blew his friend through the storefront glass of a local pizza restaurant just a short walk from our home.

Though many of my friends and schoolmates lived in these gang-infested neighborhoods, also mere blocks from my house, we tended to stay tightly knit in our associations and activities. We surfed Huntington Beach every Sunday and, after school, our skateboard endeavors rivaled the kids from Venice Beach. Our street survival skills were few and simple: avoid certain streets after dark, and never make extended eye contact with gang members who would stare us down as we road our skateboards past notorious places like the gritty Tanapa Pool Hall.

We weren't aware of it at the time, but choosing the right friends and activities turns out to be the single most important self-defense move you can make when it comes to avoiding violence. Statistically speaking, if you are white, in your fifties, well educated, and living in an upscale neighborhood with great schools and a low crime rate, you match the characteristics of a person who is at very low risk of a violent attack. On the other hand, if you are a 15-year-old black male from a disadvantaged neighborhood, you are statistically at the highest risk of violent victimization. Common knowledge might dictate the same, except, it doesn't exactly work that way.

FBI crime statistics across the country—and over the

years—demonstrate that victimization from violence has far less to do with age, race, and socioeconomic status, and far more to do with who you associate with and what activities you choose to occupy your days and nights. In other words, your chances of being involved in a violent encounter are more controlled by *what you do* than by who you are.[16] If the 15-year-old chooses his friends wisely and spends most school evenings doing homework, his chances of violent crime victimization drop dramatically. If the educated, affluent, white male regularly trolls the county park at midnight for prostitutes or drugs, his chances of being a victim of violent crime are now statistically higher than the street-smart black teen from the disadvantaged neighborhood.

———

If you believe this section of the book doesn't apply to you—maybe because you don't "hang around with the wrong crowd," or you're not a member of a street gang—look for a moment at the broader spectrum of activities or actions you undertake. Intentionally or not, these may invoke a violent response. It happens all the time. Someone having an affair should be expected to be confronted by an enraged spouse if discovered, and while this spouse may never have had a self-control or anger management issue previously, his or her first reaction in this instance could very well be homicidal. Or maybe your activities find you either supporting or confronting people with extreme viewpoints at heated rallies or protests, or lobbing insults at the other team's fans or players, or if you're the one with the road rage (if you're the aggressor), be forewarned. I am not telling you how to live your life in this book, but I am telling you that much of the violence in this world is self-inflicted and avoidable.

SELF-INFLICTED TROUBLE

Perhaps it seems obvious, but self-discipline or self-control is vitally important when it comes to your ability to dictate your own fate in certain situations. Admittedly, it is difficult to maintain one's composure when facing individuals who are disruptive, rude, drunk, belligerent, aggressive, or the like. It is! You can feel the rage bubble up inside you, and the temptation to formally introduce your fist into this guy's jaw is palpable. At these times, however, remember that "let cooler heads prevail" became a lasting adage for a reason. You control 100% of your actions and reactions. As difficult as it is to hear someone berating your team, having someone purposely cut you off on the highway, or even flirting with your significant other, you control how you respond. You will achieve a feeling of calmness, become more comfortable with yourself, and gain confidence when you choose not to let anyone get to you.

Another way to look at it is: you can't control other people anyway, so why bother? Seriously, have you ever heard someone acknowledge that they are a loud, obnoxious jerk, thank the other person for the confrontation, and confess they were now going to change their personality?

Realize that this person will forever be this way, so it really is up to you to maintain control of yourself and to not cross the line. It falls upon you to keep your emotions in check. The best way to handle these challenging or difficult individuals is to walk away from them, ignore them, and, perhaps, smile to yourself in satisfaction that you did not cause a situation to escalate and result in who knows what kind of damage, injury, or arrest. Again, I realize that choosing not to confront these individuals is hard to do. In these situations, where some of you will feel you have some sort of manly duty to engage (and you believe you run the risk of looking like a coward if you don't), drop it and move on. Not taking the bait is always the wisest decision.

Only on rare occasions would I suggest doing something more. This is typically when the individual(s) are physically in your space or blocking your path of travel and you are faced with no alternative. Here, you may have no choice except to engage, but do it verbally, not physically, at first. Follow the lesson police are taught: use small words and don't say a lot. An example would be, "Please move." And, of course, maintain your composure when engaging. If the other person is making direct eye contact with you and still refuses to step aside, I would consider that an immediate threat to you with the potential for serious bodily harm. Legally, you can inflict sufficient pain on the jerk to cause him to comply with your request.

IF FEAR BECOMES YOUR FOCUS

There is absolutely nothing wrong with having rational fear. It keeps us from doing otherwise stupid things. Rational fear keeps us from stepping out on a 100-story ledge to feed the birds. It keeps us from driving on a dark desert highway when low on fuel, or from walking down a poorly lit alley at night. It even keeps us from walking into a biker bar and ordering a Shirley Temple on the rocks with extra cherries! Basically, it's pre-wired in all of us and keeps us safe and out of harm's way. It's listening to our gut instincts, and, in the context of this book, it helps us from becoming victimized if we trust our intuitive sense to help keep us from risky and questionable, if not outright perilous, situations.

However, if fear becomes your focus, it's an unhealthy fear. If your fear makes you more cautious than you really need to be to stay safe, or completely paralyzes you from taking the action you should be taking when threatened, it's a fear you need to overcome. I'm not referring to certain irrational fears, like never leaving your house because you're convinced something bad will happen to you, or phobias, like Arachnophobia (fear of spiders) or Ophidiophobia (fear of snakes). These are examples of anxiety disorders that are best treated with therapy and are not in my scope of expertise.

I'm talking primarily about the fear of fighting, which is not a disorder or an irrational fear; it's normal. Intelligent, well-adjusted people don't generally like to fight. Why? There's the fear of physical pain and injury and the fear of possible humiliation (if you get pounded in front of your girlfriend or classmates). Both are bound to raise your heartbeat and knot up your stomach from nerves. The toughest boxers and MMA fighters in the world will tell you they get nervous before a fight, even to the point of vomiting. Champions, though, learn to channel their anxiety into focused, controlled aggression by achieving (in various ways) an almost Zen-like calmness—not just before the fight, but also throughout it.

If, when encountering any threatening person, your fear is so intense that your mind and body become overwhelmed, you'll absolutely fail to defend yourself or others who depend on you, and it's time to make some changes. First up is learning to channel the fear, and the unfamiliar feelings of the adrenaline rush you experience in a confrontation, into an unmatched surge of energy, confidence, and action. Like championship fighters, you can learn to calm your nerves and leverage fear to your advantage.

OVERCOMING FEAR

People worry more about violence and crime if they think they're physically vulnerable. It makes sense. Except, research has shown those who think they're in poor health, regardless of whether they actually are, also feel like they're more likely to be victimized by criminals. In other words, if you *feel* vulnerable, then you *are* vulnerable. Your attitude and demeanor alone have turned you into a soft target for criminals or predators, enabling a self-fulfilling prophecy. What does that say about the mindset of a person when it comes to overcoming fear or fighting back? Maybe you've given up entirely on the option to protect yourself because you think you can't. There are other explanations (or excuses) that keep people from fighting back, including smaller size and strength, a lack of training, a lack of conviction to fight back, and being overwhelmed by nerves and the adrenaline pumping through the body. If any of these sound familiar to you, here are four ways you can overcome those fears.

Lacking Size and Strength

Wing Chun, the only mainstream martial art created by a woman, has been a huge influence on me and is integral to my personal defense system. This centuries-old martial art was created by Ng Moi, a small, frail Buddhist nun who specifically designed the fighting system to counter her lack of size and strength. If you're a smaller person, or lack strength or athleticism, you may be surprised to learn how much pain you can inflict on an attacker, even a much bigger and stronger one, using Wing Chun techniques, or many others. I warn my students regularly to watch out for the smaller person you may engage—it's an advantage for the opponent some people don't think about. Shorter men and women are lower to the ground, giving them excellent balance. And they often take up wrestling or Jiu-Jitsu in high school or later. If trained, they'll shoot for your legs, wrap you up, and have you flat on your back before you ever knew what hit you. The next thing you know, they're sitting on your chest backwards, immobilizing you with their ankles wrapped around your leg and neck, and torqueing your knee in the wrong direction, causing immense pain and serious injury if you don't submit. You can defend against ground fighters with anti-grappling techniques but it takes practice. Additionally, shorter persons can make themselves even smaller by lowering their weight, tucking their head and chin, and covering their head or body with their arms, offering very few targets to strike cleanly. Being smaller than average has its advantages in a violent encounter and it should not be a reason to fear confrontation.

A lighter weight person can fight effectively if they know where and how to strike to maximize pain, avoid being taken to the ground, and utilize their speed to escape after initially stunning an attacker. One of the best weapons a slight person holds is that bad guys never expect them to fight back. When they do, with a fury of speedy eye jabs, throat punches, nose crushers, and knees and kicks to the body, the assailant is caught completely by surprise and is disoriented enough to allow for the target's escape. That is, if the assailant doesn't run away himself first!

A non-athletic person may be intimidated by the idea of self-protection training. They may have it in their mind that inflicting physical pain on someone, or anyone, is a fantasy, but that's not usually the case. While some non-athletic people find the very idea of fighting itself terrifying, I have had non-athletic students of various sizes, ages, and weights who have come alive and thrived when they discovered, say, how effective they are at stopping or slowing a taller, stronger opponent. (And they love releasing their pent-up stress on the heavy bags and practice dummies, many throwing a real punch for the first time in their lives.)

No Fight Experience or Training

Remember your first job, getting your driver's license, or even a first date? You were probably nervous and a little afraid—like most of us were. After driving for years, dating many times, and moving onto more challenging jobs, you naturally got better and more comfortable with each of these endeavors. It's no different with self-protection. The more fighting skills you learn and the more repetitions you complete, the more natural your instincts will develop. Actions and reactions start to happen swiftly and powerfully without you even thinking about them. This, in turn, leads to quiet confidence, and confidence builds self-esteem. You'll look like a more formidable opponent to those unaware of your skills without ever throwing a punch in their presence. Predators and bullies will wait for less confident prey just by sizing up the lack of fear and intimidation in your demeanor. Start slow and gradually work your skill level up to meet your goals—but start! You wouldn't drive a car without some practice, and you don't want a violent encounter to be the first time you've ever thrown a serious punch.

Conviction

All the boxing or martial arts training in the world won't help you in a violent encounter if you lack the conviction to fight back. I'd place much better odds on the survival of the untrained person who didn't hesitate to unleash everything they had, as fast as they could attack, against a criminal predator than someone with self-defense training who lacked confidence in their fighting abilities. If you don't believe you can defeat your enemy, you probably won't. Conviction comes from a properly developed self-defense mindset (which I previously discussed), and the foundation of that mindset is confidence, which comes from training and practice.

Controlling Adrenaline and Nerves

It seems counterintuitive to teach people to relax before they attack someone who may be trying to seriously injure or kill them. In a real-world situation, your acute stress response system (fight or flight response) automatically floods your body and brain with a surge of hormones designed to temporarily increase strength and alertness. Along with this comes an increased heartbeat, rapid breathing, and trembling arms and legs (the result of blood flow being redirected by your brain to protect your vital organs). In addition to this involuntary response by your brain is a common *voluntary* fighting ritual, where untrained people who face the possibility of a fight focus on getting themselves "keyed up"—too keyed up—which leads to increased muscular tension, poor decision-making, loss of concentration, and disrupted rhythm and coordination. Planting your feet like they were hardened into the concrete and stiffening your arms and legs in anticipation of physical contact is one of the worst things you can do because your tension is easy to turn against you. Knowing how to stay calm and relaxed before and during a fight will not only convey an intimidating air of confidence to your opponent, but it will improve your reflexes, power, balance, and stamina. When you learn to repurpose fear and adrenaline, rather than be overwhelmed by it, you now have a powerful advantage.

Staying calm in the heat of battle requires a burst of

intense focus on the singular task of confronting and defeating your opponent. Equally important is controlling your stress, anger, and ego in everyday situations. It's vital to your overall health and well-being, and it quiets the hair trigger impulses to instigate, escalate, or overreact with unwarranted physical violence. How to induce calm under pressure is the subject of our next chapter.

4

MANGING DAILY STRESS AND EGO THROUGH MINDFULNESS

We all live in a continuous state of stress, most of the time without being aware of it. It becomes more obvious when the demands of life, family, relationships, school, or work exceed our ability to cope. We have daily things that affect all of us differently, sometimes simply depending on outlook. The long, heavily congested commute to work is a significant stressor for some, for instance, but to others it's a welcome break for themselves where they can listen to their favorite music or podcasts, or simply use the time for quiet reflection *true!* or creative thinking. Whatever the source, stress triggers poor decision-making; it makes our egos seem more fragile, setting us off into a rage even for minor incidents of perceived disrespect, sometimes with brutal consequences.

Some stress is good for us, such as motivating us to finish a major project or cram for a big exam, or the physiological response from our bodies own acute stress response, discussed earlier. Developed and evolved since the days of

the early humans, the acute stress response is an instanta-
neous dose of mega-stress that drives our body's fight or
flight mechanism, helping to protect us in life-threatening
situations. It's what gives us a split-second reaction time to an
oncoming car collision, or the intense focus and burst of
super energy and stamina to run or fight when we detect an
imminent physical threat.

However, chronic stress (living with a heightened state of
stress most of the time) can lead to serious health conditions,
including anxiety, insomnia, muscle pain, digestive and
reproductive issues, memory impairment, high blood pressure, and a weakened immune system. Untreated, chronic
stress can contribute to the development of major illnesses,
such as heart disease, depression, and obesity. In extreme
cases, chronic stress is often the underlying significant
trigger that causes someone to "snap" and murder a stranger
in a fit of rage or someone they know in a crime of passion.

For years, mental health experts have been advising us to
combat stress and reduce anxiety with exercise, laughter, and
talking to friends or family about the sources of stress in our
lives. Experts also recommend stepping away from the
stressor (the stimulus causing the stress) as an effective stress
reduction technique. This chapter focuses on stepping away
from your stressors because it is every bit as critical to self-
protection as anything you'll learn from this book. Why? It
comes down to two fundamentals of how you respond to a
potentially violent encounter: overcoming fear and self-
control. Both fundamentals need to be cultivated within your
personal defense mindset and ultimately drawn upon in
times of an escalating crisis.

The concept of overcoming fear was touched on in the last chapter, but self-control is the other bookend. Self-control keeps you from being the source of the dangerous behavior in the first place; it prevents stress, anger, passion, or intoxicants from triggering an irrational response to a provocation from someone else. The mindset of self-control teaches you to ignore confrontational people and attendant situations, and it becomes equally valuable in preventing an overreaction should you engage, as these may escalate to excessive use of force, and with it, the potential for serious criminal charges and civil suits against you.

Let's take a closer look at the benefits of stepping away from your stressors before we get into *how* to step away from your stressors. And when it comes to self-inflicted stressors, one above all is responsible for so many unnecessary assaults, injuries, and deaths: the unhinged ego.

Your unhinged ego is the reason you fly off the handle when something doesn't go your way, or why you become overly aggressive if someone disrespects you. Guys, I'm mainly speaking to you right now. Let me be blunt: what makes you so damn important? Why do you expect such treatment or entitlement? Maybe you need to examine your own fragile ego to help you answer these questions. Don't put it off. Keeping your ego in check may save your life someday. The unhinged ego is the source of road rage, bar fights, the murder of ex-girlfriends or spouses, gangland slayings, and countless other assaults and deaths. Egoism taken to an extreme is behind mass shootings (UC Santa Barbara), serial killings (The Golden State Killer) and assassinations (John Lennon).

When you can clear your mind briefly and routinely from the things that are bringing you stress and anxiety, not only is it medically proven to lower your blood pressure, reduce your heart rate, and induce a beneficial calming effect on your body, it brings into focus the things and people most important to you. This, in turn, is vital to your ability to make split-second decisions on when to "flip the switch" and engage in a potential conflict or threat, or when to walk away. You will know instantly how to discern between mindless, ego-driven violence and a serious threat to you or someone you love, or someone who is being victimized by violence and needs your help. This mindfulness causes hesitation to disappear, and the critical few seconds needed to act aren't squandered on uncertainty. However, if an abundance of personal stress is driving your decision-making, you run the risk of reacting out of ego to a meaningless act of disrespect, or acting indecisively in instances of legitimate necessity.

Fear is another source of stress. Real fear is a good thing. It's what causes you to hit the brakes before crashing into the car in front of you without even thinking about it. However, psychological fear, which stems from our ego and our inse-curities, is not healthy. It manifests itself in anger, hostility, complaints, and negativity. The longer your ego thinks about a real or perceived injustice, the more that voice in your head talks to itself about it. It begins to create a victim identity around it, expanding it into a story to be told to others, and the more personal the story becomes, the more anxious and bruised your ego feels. Getting your out-of-balance ego back into balance is one of the major reasons I use and teach my students a breathing and focus practice called "Qigong" (pronounced: gee-gung). Qigong teaches us how to step away from our stressors.

QIGONG

Qigong was commonly called "Chi Kung" until about 30 years ago (the change occurred in the 1950's when Communist China adopted pinyin over Mandarin, the former language used). But the teachings of Qigong are thousands of years old, and literally thousands of types of Qigong exist. For the purposes of this book, though, I am only going to discuss one.

I like to use the word "energy" when I teach Qigong. As Albert Einstein recognized and famously stated, *"Everything is energy, and that's all there is to it."* Because everything is, well, everything—the proverbial "whole enchilada"—this includes our thoughts. Our thoughts are the energy, or "Qi" (pronounced: chee), that flows throughout our body, and our thoughts create our reality. Most Qigong practitioners call Qi the "life energy," and every living thing has Qi.

Qigong is more about physics than philosophy (and does not encompass nor conflict with any religious beliefs). By learning how to simply stop, breathe, and relax, you are practicing Qigong. I will admit that I was a skeptic at first. After all, my father was a medical doctor, and I was raised believing Western medicine was the panacea—that shots, surgery, and pills provided the path to health. I also work in construction, so I'm not what you would call a "New Age" kind of guy. This stuff seemed "far out." The idea of Qi? The importance of balance and harmony with the mind and body? Really???

But on the other hand, I was reading testimonial after testimonial heaping praise on Qigong and its benefits. This was long before the days of claims of "fake news," but regardless, there were just too many of them to have been fake. So, I kept an open mind and began to practice Qigong. Honestly, at first, I was not impressed. But through persistence and daily practice, and as I allowed my mind to empty and started to connect my mind and body, I could not believe what I was experiencing. With utter astonishment, I felt the instant benefits of inner peace and acceptance of myself as well as the shedding of my ego's psychological fears.

Yes, learning how to breathe to cultivate my Qi through my body's meridians seemed akin to witchcraft, but I can't begin to tell you how much my daily practice of Qigong positively affects my health and life. Without a doubt, there is a leap of faith involved when you believe there is this "vital energy" called Qi running through our bodies, but I related it to "The Force" in "Star Wars." At least then I could conceptualize what "The Force" could be, and I focused my thoughts on controlling this "energy" in my body...and it worked!

You experience true Qi in different ways, but most typically, you'll feel warmth in your body and a slight tingling sensation. Qigong induces a calm and deeply relaxed state of mind and also energizes you as you are practicing and thereafter. Even after a short five-minute Qigong practice session (we will be starting with a five-minute practice because everyone can spare five minutes), you will start to feel the effects. You'll feel *relaxed*. My hope is that you will like it so much that you will build up to a whopping 15-minute practice (that's right, Qigong is still not going to take a huge time commitment on your part, and you can always decide to stick to the five-minute practice). Then you will really feel warmer, deeply relaxed, and more energetic, with greater clarity in your thoughts and actions! This is the Qi!

Again, these consequences are because Qi is an expression energy—our body's energy—resulting from what I call the "Qi Paradigm." You don't need to understand Qi to sense it and reap its benefits, but you do need to believe that your body and mind are interconnected (in fact, when you think of Qi, just imagine the visual imprint of energy in your body). The belief of Qi is like the belief in our sixth sense (which we all have). Part of the Qi Paradigm is the practice of quieting your mind and living in the present. Accept who you are and *like* let go of past experiences which cause your stress and anxi- *Tolstoy's* ety. And do not worry about any future events...the constant *concepts* worry of what is going to happen is what cripples us.

This is the essence of MINDFULNESS. Living in the present makes us aware of what is currently around us, which is the main point. We need to let go of our busy minds, ridding them of the constant stream of thoughts and visions that cause us to stray away from any true calmness or deep relaxation. In my opinion, stress is the disease of our modern day living. Our health has taken a beating because of the overwhelming stress of today. All types of exercise can help with stress, but it is not enough. Qigong provides that additional element, that deep relaxation that up until recently few westerners had ever experienced. Qigong is the perfect way to combat stress and anxiety. The energy you'll receive is not a stimulant nor akin to an adrenaline rush; it is a relaxed inner calm that comes from the mind-body connection.

Oh, and by the way, Qigong also leads to better sleep even if you practice it in the morning. I haven't had to take any kind of sleeping aids for years.

PRACTICING QIGONG

Okay, enough about the benefits. Here's how to practice Qigong.

Qigong can be practiced virtually anywhere and at any time of the day or night because its effects are lasting. Still, try to find yourself as quiet a place as possible. That's why people tend to do their practice in the morning, when the world tends to be more at peace. People also tend to practice in the morning because studies show that's when we're most energized, which is why a good number of sports teams practice first thing in the morning. And in China, they practice first thing in the morning because air pollution is at its lowest level for the day. That said, a short Qigong practice is recommended anytime you're feeling stressed, and it is a great way to revitalize yourself if you're feeling tired in the afternoon, much akin to a power nap. It truly doesn't matter when you practice.

Next, turn off or silence all external stimuli, such as televisions and cellphones (you may want to simply turn off your cell phone's ringer if you want to use your phone as your timer).

Stand with your feet at shoulder width apart, ʒ
slightly pointed inwards one to two inches and your
a comfortable bend (3-4 inches). Now start to relax. As you're
relaxing, pretend that a string is holding your head high, but
that your head is floating effortlessly above your neck (you
don't want your head to drop during the practice). As for
your arms and hand, with elbows bent, your positioning
should look like you're holding an imaginary volleyball out
in front of you (your hands should be that far apart, with
your fingers spread and grasping the imaginary ball). Start to
roll your hips slightly forward as if you're on the edge of a
barstool. This straightens your spine, which is of utmost
importance. Now relax and drop your shoulders and, with
lips barely opened and a loose jaw, start breathing through
your nose.

Breathe calm and steady, but take deeper breaths than
normal. Our body's typical involuntary inhale/exhale takes
about 2-4 seconds. We're looking to double that time here, a
5-6 second inhale/exhale. But don't force it; it's not like we're
trying to expand our lungs just prior to holding our breath
underwater. Eventually, we'd like to build up to a 10-second
inhalation, with a 10-second exhalation (roughly tripling our
normal breath). But initially, just try to double your normal
breath and, without timing it, try to make the length or pace
of your inhale about the same length or pace of your exhale.
When you think that you've inhaled for whatever time you're
shooting for, exhale until you think the right amount of time
has passed. There is no right or wrong.

While breathing, keep your eyes slightly open, gazing
softly ahead of you (the point is relaxation, not falling asleep,

and you're not focusing on anything other than your breathing). Also, keeping your eyes slightly open will help keep you from being distracted, which tends to happen when we open our eyes widely. And while breathing, place the tip of your tongue gently on your upper palate (I know it sounds strange, but just trust me on this...remember, I was a skeptic too!).

Pay attention to your rhythmic breath for the first 60 to 90 seconds. Let your mind go empty outside of the singular focus on your breath. With each exhale, you'll feel more relaxed. As you're feeling more relaxed (during this 60 to 90 second period), take all of the tension in your body and envision pushing all of it down to your feet (think like sand in an hourglass), then through your feet and into the ground below you.

> Note: After a couple of sessions, you will find yourself not paying attention to your breath during these first 60 to 90 seconds and you will go into an "auto mode" of feeling relaxed and pushing out your tensions. You will feel the equilibrium in your balance, and maintaining this correct posture, known as "Zhan Zhuang" (pronounced: Jan Jong), or the standing meditation pose, will take only minimal effort.

So far, so good? Again, I hate using terms like "meditation" for fear of turning some people off. But who cares what anything's called if it works, right? It's like enjoying sushi before you know what it really is, and then saying, "Who cares? It's delicious."

Now, envision your breath as a little ball of light. As you inhale, feel it coming up from your "Dantian," which is the center of our breathing and balance and located 2-3 inches below your navel. Feel it reach the top of your head, then exhale and, like the drop of the ball at midnight on New Year's Eve, feel the ball travel back down to the Dantian, completing a cycle. Continue this pattern of envisioning while breathing, where you are holistically connecting the body and brain for whatever time remains in your session. At the end of the session, take ten breaths, each of the same duration as the others in this session.

As I said, we'll start with a daily five-minute practice. Maybe do it at the same time every day so that you won't forget to do it, so you'll establish some sort of routine. After a week or two, increase the practice to ten minutes. Then, after another week or two, as you continue to feel the benefits, increase your session to fifteen minutes. Again, this is the daily routine, and if you feel fifteen minutes is or will be too much, stick to five minutes. I promise, you'll still feel relaxed and it will help with your circulation. That all said, feel free to add in another session or two whenever you're feeling stressed, anxious, or fatigued.

———

I don't just teach Qigong for mindfulness, stress reduction, and repairing out-of-balance egos. The benefits of controlled breathing are essential to staying focused and calm while fighting an opponent. Hyperventilating—or the opposite, not breathing at all—is common in untrained people who are attacked. In fact, almost all of my students who begin micro sparring (creating simulated stress under attack) either breathe too fast (getting lightheaded and dizzy) or forget to breathe altogether! Controlled, even breathing promotes calm and delivers necessary oxygen to the bloodstream. Calmness, while striking and kicking at a bad guy, is critical to your speed, power, and accuracy. And a relaxed, balanced stance when fighting makes it difficult for your opponent to use your own strength against you, whereas a rigid and tense fighter is easily pushed off balance. As an added benefit, your staying calm in a fight literally freaks the opponent out. Unless they're trained at fighting themselves, you're quickly going to get into their head.

Whatever your personal reasons may be for learning and practicing Qigong, whether you are 15 or 90 years old, all I can say is: just try it!

Qigong Practice Quick Reference

1. Choose a quiet location.

2. Stand with feet shoulder width apart and toes pointed a few inches inward.

3. Bend at the knees several inches.

4. Hold both arms out in front of you, with elbows near your hips, and lightly grip an imaginary tree or volleyball.

5. Straighten your spine and relax your shoulders.

6. Breathe in deep (about 90%) through your nose and out from your mouth. Try for slow, even, rhythmic breaths.

7. Imagine your breath as a ball of light continuously circling in from your Dantian and out through the top of your head, and in sync with your breathing. Start with a daily 5-minute practice session.

8. End the session with 10 consecutive breaths, each of them equal in duration to the others in your session.

My Qigong instructional videos can be found at www.defensekinetics.com

PART II

THE OUTSIDE SPHERE OF SELF-PROTECTION

Ten-year-old Julianna Osso was sitting in two feet of water at a designated swimming area at Orlando Florida's Moss Park on May 8, 2017, when an alligator suddenly attacked her, clamping down on her leg at least seven times. Her family and the lifeguard on duty pulled the young girl to shore and rushed her to the hospital. Miraculously, she survived the gator attack with only a few minor injuries.

But Julianna wasn't just lucky, she was prepared. She forced the alligator to open its jaws and release her leg by using a trick she'd learned months before, on a class field trip to a local wildlife preserve. Turns out, as demonstrated by a gator handler at the preserve, if you stick your fingers in an alligator's nose, it will reflexively open its jaws. In this terrifying moment, Julianna first tried hitting the gator on its forehead to escape, but with no success. Then, she remembered the wrangler's technique. "I was scared at first, but I knew what to do," Julianna said. She then plunged two fingers into the gator's nostrils, blocking its airway. The gator's jaws instantly sprung open and Julianna freed her leg.

Some very respectable self-defense experts like to make it a point that techniques are only useful for those who are professionally trained. Everyone else, they say, will forget what to do in the panic and confusion of a real-life attack. For this reason, they advise ordinary people to stick with basic principles of survival rather than specific techniques to thwart an assailant. For Julianna, I guess this would be the equivalent of "stay out of the water," or maybe "use your hands with opposing force to quickly snap the gator's leg at the joint in the opposite direction it was intended to move, and with sufficient force to cause the ligaments to tear." Sorry, but a 10-year-old had both the mindset and quick thinking to deliver a simple technique to escape the clenches of a nine-foot alligator! If she can do it, you can do it.

Mindset is 99% of engaging an assailant. Having an overwhelming confidence in your ability to replicate the techniques you will learn in Part Two (with practice and repetition with a partner) will allow you to act without doubt, without any moral ambiguity, and without any hesitation. You will be confident that not only can you attack, but you can also attack with ferocity. You will be able to become violent and act with total conviction if such need ever arises, embracing and utilizing to your advantage your adrenaline surge. You'll be able to inflict severe pain and bring unexpected and unwanted attention to a violent encounter, which are the only two fears assailants understand. In fact, your mindset will not be one of protecting yourself. You will be the one on the attack, responding to violence with violence. Your once violent predator becomes your prey. *Hmmm,,,*

And so, it is with this mindset that we begin the *Outside* sphere of *Inside-Out Self-Protection*, which is where the fists start flying, weapons may come into play, and serious consequences are in the mix, including your own personal liability and avoiding jail for your actions. Exactly what you can (and cannot) do to legally defend yourself, or others, is one of the most misunderstood topics in self-protection. For this reason, I'll start with a story and a discussion on the (often misunderstood) laws of self-defense.

5

THE LAW OF SELF-DEFENSE

Okay, so what can you do when escape is not an option—when your awareness of the people and situation around you give you the sense something bad may potentially happen with nowhere to run or hide? Or what if an unseen character with evil intent suddenly and surprisingly appears and you're trapped?

When I was eleven, a friend and I decided to take the RTD bus, now called the Metro, to Seal Beach. We didn't care that the ride took two and a half hours in each direction or that the bus's last stop still put us a mile's walk to and from the ocean. Nope, we wanted a day of adventure and boogie boarding, and this was the way to do it. If a preteen road trip sounds far-fetched, it was 1980. Things were different then, and by this time my mom was no longer around, leaving my unconventional and preoccupied father to raise three kids alone. I could've taken a bus to Mexico and he would've been fine with it (and puzzled at why I asked permission). Left to our own entertainment and travel planning, my friend and I completely overlooked the fact that the bus would be traveling through some rough neighborhoods.

After a great day at the beach, my friend and I hopped on the bus at 4:30 for the return ride home. Exhausted and with boogie boards in hand, we plopped into seats about two rows from the back of the bus, and while not thrilled about how long the return trip home would take, we were looking forward to a mellow ride. The atmosphere changed about an hour later when six gang members stepped onto the bus, although "stepped onto" sounds way too civil. At once, they were rude to the driver by refusing to pay and throwing expletives his way as he protested their actions and non-payment. Working their way down the aisle, they took to knocking hats off some passengers and accosting others, with more swearing at an even greater volume. Their twenty-something leader, the one who led the procession down the aisle, was the most vocal of all.

The leader had just woken a slumbering 40-year-old man by smacking him in the face when he locked eyes with me, looking every bit the 11-year-old that I was, complete with red hair and freckles. The leader strutted towards me with an arrogant laugh. Stopping a foot away, he yelled something incoherent and then suddenly lunged towards me...What could I do? Did I have a right to strike him first?

Set aside for the moment that I was a preteen. Child, adolescent, or adult, the simple answer is "yes," though it's important to understand that the law governing self-defense has never been as simple as excusing any violent act just because another person hit you first. Traditionally, self-defense laws have required someone being attacked by another to act reasonably, so a successful self-defense claim required showing that the defendant had no other choice—he couldn't defuse the situation by using less force or safely walk away from the aggressor. And on the specific point of safely walking away, in today's world, nearly one in four states insist that you have a legal duty to retreat, to walk away if possible instead of physically engaging a potential threat. Other states allow you to "stand your ground," regardless of your ability to just walk away, and virtually all states recognize that the rules change significantly if someone breaks into your home. The so-called "Castle Doctrine" is an exception to the laws described above, which allow people who are in their own homes more freedom to use violence against aggressors or intruders. This doctrine is based on the age-old notion that "a man's home is his castle," and it permits a person to use even deadly force against someone who has entered his home without permission and who poses an imminent threat of serious injury. The defense does not involve any consideration of whether retreat was safely possible. In some states, the resident can use violence even if the intruder wasn't using or threatening serious force.

Even though it varies from state to state, all states have laws that provide a basic "self-defense" defense—when you've committed an offense of some sort, but your response is justifiable if reasonable under the circumstances, whether inside or outside of your "castle." And where the punches, kicks, or your hit over the attacker's head with a candlestick provides you with self-protection, the "self-defense" defense provides you with legal protection.

First, though, just what offense have you possibly committed? More than likely, unless death has occurred, you've committed battery. Battery is typically where you intend harmful or offensive contact with another person, and you follow through with that contact. Some states include contact that results from recklessness or criminal negligence, and it is doesn't matter that you didn't intend the harm; what matters is whether you intended the contact. If you intend the contact and the contact happens, you're potentially guilty or liable, and if death results, then you're looking at some sort of charge of a homicide like murder, voluntary manslaughter, or involuntary manslaughter.

Yet, under certain circumstances, it is legally justifiable to commit such offenses. Again, each state has its own definition, but a claim of self-defense is universally recognized.

Let's look at the general definition of self-defense and then break it down. I promise you that after it's broken down, it's a lot less complicated than, say, what constitutes a catch in the NFL.

Generally, an individual is justified in repelling what they reasonably believe to be an imminent assault by the exercise of such reasonable force as may be, or appears at the time to be, necessary to protect oneself from bodily harm.

Huh? In reading this you were probably thinking that this is exactly why you didn't go to law school. Still, even in a cursory reading, perhaps you noticed that there was some sort of "reasonableness" afoot. After all, the word "reasonable" was used twice, and there was also something else about "imminent." Well, in a nutshell, there you have it. Generally, so long as you're reasonable in your response because you reasonably believed something was about to happen to you, you're okay in using self-defense.

That's good, but what does the law consider "reasonable"? There are hundreds of years' worth of court cases about whether individuals acted reasonably under their given circumstances or reasonably thought they were about to be hurt by another. Mind you, the individual just had to reasonably believe they were going to be hurt, they did not actually have to suffer any injury. And acting reasonably under the circumstances, including the amount of force an individual used when they thought they were about to be hurt, almost always turns on common sense. A judge or a jury under deliberation will always ask himself or herself: would a reasonable person standing in their shoes have acted the same way? This includes even if there was some error in judgment at that time.

Fortunately, common sense also comes into play as to the question: what is considered "imminent"? Again, an individual reasonably needs to believe that the assault against them is going to be imminent in order to be justified in using self-defense. They don't need for the assault to happen or wait to be attacked; they just need to reasonably believe that an assault is going to happen before they can legally defend themselves. Again, would a reasonable person standing in their shoes reasonably believe an assault was imminent?

Stand Your Ground

However, as I mentioned previously, a newer trend in self-defense, known as the "stand your ground" doctrine, has arisen recently in many states, effectively lowering the bar for a legal self-defense claim for those who use force against a threatening person. In short, the new stand your ground statutes do not require the person being attacked to retreat whatsoever, even if they can. Some of these laws, such as Florida's, specifically state that a person being attacked or threatened, even in a public place, "has the right to stand his or her ground" and meet force with force. The stand your ground defense played a part in the 2013 Florida prosecution of George Zimmerman, accused of second-degree murder of the unarmed teenager Travon Martin. In some states, however, the stand your ground doctrine only applies to non-lethal self-defense. Today, 32 states have adopted some form of the stand your ground defense, while other states have retained traditional self-defense statutes that limit the right of self-defense to certain actions in certain circumstances.

———

Let's go back to me on that bus for a moment. Did I have the right to use deadly force against the gang leader who lunged at me? The answer is: could a reasonable person in my position feel he was about to use deadly force against me? Generally, an individual can only use that amount of force equal to the amount necessary to subdue the perceived threat. So, if someone is threatening you with a gun, generally, you can respond with deadly force. On the other hand, if someone is threatening you with a feather, you'll have a very tough time justifying the use of deadly force. In any event, if it's clear that the threat of deadly force against you no longer exists, your legal right to use deadly force in response no longer exists. In fact, if any threat of harm no longer exists, you must legally cease the use of any previous force. In other words, even if you've turned the tables, you can't keep pummeling someone once they've clearly been subdued. There are, of course, exceptions to the above. We've already talked about some states that allow individuals to use deadly force at any time to protect their homes against unlawful entrants (and these same laws apply to the workplace and to land, depending on the State).

Returning to my situation, I think you'll agree that I was trapped on that bus. With nowhere to go, I could not have "retreated" if I wanted to, regardless of whatever my state's law happened to have been. I'll tell you now that I didn't use deadly force, but could I have justified its use as I posed earlier? The leader had not drawn a gun, nor any weapon, but I would argue, yes. A reasonable person in my position at that time could have honestly believed—and it was objectively reasonable to conclude, under the circumstances— that I was about to suffer great bodily harm. By contrast, substitute a group of harmless-looking Boy Scouts for the gang members, and a scout leader for the gang leader, who backed off after a few choice words shouted in my direction, then sat back down. The fact pattern changes completely, along with any reasonable self-defense legal claim for striking the scout leader first, much less the use of deadly force.

Defense of Property

But the above discussion, as well as the discussion that follows, is about whether the legal right to strike first exists if I feel I'm in imminent danger of serious bodily harm. What if it's my property the guy wants instead? What if the gang leader, instead of lunging towards me, lunged towards my boogie board? As I mentioned before, you have a right to defend your home and land, both of which are referred to as "real property." What about any right to defend "personal property" (moveable objects) like boogie boards? In most states, I have the right to use reasonable force to protect my boogie board if I have a reasonable belief that an imminent threat of damage, destruction, or theft will occur. In general, most states do not authorize the use of deadly force to protect property (other than the home) under any circumstances.

So, if I reasonably believed the gang leader, by his lunge and prior actions, was going for my boogie board instead of me, and had I, say, tackled him to prevent him from doing so, I have probably used reasonable force under the circumstances and can claim defense of property as my defense for battery. If the gang leader claims that he was simply lunging towards it to get a closer look, my attack could still be justified, as it was reasonable for me to believe that the gang leader was about to damage my property and force was immediately necessary to protect my personal property in this situation. Again, if I pull out a gun and shoot the gang leader, I could not claim defense of property because deadly force is never justifiable to ~~protect personal property~~ (outside of your home) from harm.

What if the gang leader, in lunging towards my boogie board, had successfully grabbed it and darted down the aisle prior to me employing any force to defend my property? Most states allow an individual to chase someone who steals their personal property and use force to take the item back, so long as, generally, there is an uninterrupted flow of events.

Could I have been justified in using force if the gang members had caused no trouble at all upon entering the bus, but had simply looked scary? Can you imagine the precedent this would set if the validity of the use of force based solely on looks was upheld? We already discussed the adage about judging a book by its cover. Without more, the law and the adage say you can't.

———

What if I had been the one to initiate the trouble with the gang? Sorry, but if I provoked the encounter, I can't claim self-defense if I later need to use force to defend myself because of what I started. But if I clearly communicated to the gang that I was withdrawing, but they continued none-theless, a right to self-defense may be triggered at that point.

Self-Defense Law at Schools

You might find it interesting to learn though that, generally, you can forget all about what you've read in this chapter when it comes to school settings. As it currently stands, at most schools, the right to self-defense does not exist. The Student Code of Conduct, every school's behavioral bible, stipulates every move that K-12 youngsters may or may not make throughout their school day, and most schools have Zero Tolerance policies in place that prohibit students from fighting one another. With an absolute no tolerance policy in place, it no longer matters who started the fight. Even if a child is being bullied, that child cannot take matters into their own hands by way of self-defense. That child is expected to report the bullying behavior to school authorities, regardless of how impractical such reporting may be, and it is the school authorities that will then take any action, not the child using self-defense. In these instances, violation of the Zero Tolerance policy typically results in the suspension or expulsion of both students involved in the altercation—the aggressor and the one who sought to defend themselves.

This frustrated me as Dean of Discipline at a high school in Southern California. The files contained notes left by my predecessor, including complaints left by one student about being bullied by another, a known bully. Apparently, not much happened with regards to the situation prior to my arrival and soon after I arrived the bullied student stood up for himself in yet another encounter. Because fighting was not permitted on school grounds, I was instructed to suspend both kids for three days. I personally got in trouble when I only suspended the student being bullied for one day, but it was nothing compared to the nightmare that I experienced next. Following school guidelines, I suspended both students involved in the next bullying incident at my school, including a young woman who had merely defended herself from a bully. Indignant at the perceived injustice, she chose to retaliate.

Not long after I suspended the student, she falsely reported me for sending her inappropriate texts and for inappropriate physical contact. I was fingerprinted, held in a cell for hours, had my cell phone confiscated and was placed on paid leave. During the next two years I made 33 court appearances to clear my name. I burned through my entire retirement savings to pay legal bills and court costs and at one point I nearly lost custody of my own children. Despite what appeared to be an obvious motive and the questionable timing of the unfounded claims, I received no support from district officials and had to fend for myself against a tireless prosecutor looking to score a big bust. It didn't happen (broke and exhausted, I pled to a class C misdemeanor to end the matter, a violation equivalent to driving without a valid license). I soon found out that I wasn't alone.

A rise in the number of false allegations being made against teachers has been growing at alarming rates for the past decade, leaving teachers and staff afraid to assert their authority and discipline pupils where appropriate. Within months of the accusations made against me, a poll by the Association of Teachers and Lecturers (ATL) revealed that a quarter of school staff have been falsely accused of wrong-doing by a pupil – such as slapping them or other inappropriate physical contact – while one in six teachers have faced malicious allegations from the pupil's family. Half of those questioned said there had been at least one false allegation in their current school.

I believe it was right that the allegations made against me were investigated, but there has to be a more a streamlined initial process to spot those cases that clearly have no merit. The protection of children is paramount, but that should not be at the expense of the rights and the reputations of school staff. Experts say children who make false accusations may be motivated by a small incident, but for teachers that allegation could mean weeks or months on suspension as the investigation takes place. They can't contact colleagues or go into the school during that time. It's a totally isolating experience that results in many teachers never returning to their profession (including me) because of the cloud that follows them around and the enormous legal expenses required to defend themselves.

Victims of bullying as it turns out aren't confined to the student population, but include teachers and administrators who risk being assaulted, or having their careers destroyed, and even the possibility of criminal prosecution for simply carrying out their duties. As a result, the safest course of action for the staff is not to engage a problem student. Is it any wonder why so many of our schools in our country have teachers who have little or no control over discipline and disruption in the classroom?

Consequences of Zero Tolerance Policies

Then there's the story of Monica, a student who followed the rules. Monica is a junior in college who recently shared with me her story of being bullied and sexually assaulted as a high school student. Monica is all of 5'2" and 105 pounds, a young woman who she can be shy at times or surprisingly outgoing depending on her comfort level.

As a new high school student in a new town, she understandably carried herself quietly and demurely, but her attractiveness caught the attention of Chad (not his real name), the star of the high school's football team. One day Chad organized a Circle Maneuver around Monica on campus with a dozen other teammates after classes. A Circle Maneuver involves a group surrounding a victim, making escape impossible and concealing the assault from the view of others. As the circle constricted around Monica, the boys took turns running their hands down her pants and up her top. Monica felt helpless and humiliated. When the incident ended, sheer embarrassment kept her from immediately reporting the assault. Her "friends" encouraged her to forget about it. After all, the ring leader was popular (as bullies often are) and he was the football team star; punishing him would be punishing the whole football team, potentially damaging their season's win/loss record, and the school's reputation. However, Monica's boyfriend at the time, who attended another school, was understandably outraged. He demanded that she report the incident and the boys involved to her school's principal, and she complied.

The school subsequently suspended several boys involved in the assault, including Chad, from playing football for three weeks, including three Friday night games in a row. News of the incident and the suspensions reverberated throughout the campus, but there was no empathy for Monica. In fact, Monica received quite the opposite reaction. Football players, classmates, and even many of her "friends" shunned her for doing exactly what school administrators advise students to do in similar situations: reporting the incident. She was a persona non-grata—a non-person—to her classmates, alternately scorned and ignored. The entire, miserable chapter in her life convinced her that, in hindsight, fighting back at her attackers would have been far preferable to the pain of humiliation and isolation she felt by standing helpless in the circle of groping boys and reporting the incident later.

I'll be discussing techniques that 5'2" Monica could have employed to have successfully stopped the actions of the football players, and had she done so, I firmly believe that no one would have been likely to mess with her again during high school. But Monica's actions in following the rules had real-life consequences that the proponents of the Zero Tolerance policy either did not intend or ignored. And while they'll point to a 4% decline in schoolyard fights in recent years as proof that the policy works, incidents of bullying during these same years have remained virtually unchanged. Meanwhile, teen suicide attempts rose 10%, and teens that seriously considered suicide jumped by 23%. I don't know what role, if any, the Zero Tolerance policy had in contributing to these latter two statistics, but there are dozens of studies showing that bully victims are at particularly high risk for experiencing mental health issues such as anxiety and depression, and other studies confirm a strong connection between bullying and suicidal thoughts and action.[17] To a bully victim, our system that rewards the aggressor (by eliminating sole accountability for his actions, while simultaneously punishing the person who was attacked) must feel like it's designed to stack one injustice upon another. When you're told you cannot defend yourself without consequences from the very people who are charged to protect you at school, how can you help but feel a sense of hopelessness?

Zero tolerance policies on fighting may be expeditious for school administrators who aren't keen on playing investigator, judge, and jury, but at what cost? Exactly what message are we sending to the abusers and the victims? And aren't school regulations that punish a child acting to defend themselves taking away a right specifically recognized under the law?

Fortunately, more and more courts are holding that the blind enforcement of Zero Tolerance fighting policies—which do not consider a student's right to self-defense and subject victims to severe disciplinary action, such as suspension or expulsion—is unlawful. In Monica's case, she was sexually assaulted, which she might have been able to thwart by countering with the appropriate amount of violence commensurate with the threat made on her. Granted, she was not thinking, "But if I strike, I'll be suspended or expelled" at the time of the assault, nor should she have. That should never be something that needs to race through a victim's mind in that instant.

———

And so, returning to my bus ride back from Seal Beach and my 11-year-old self, what exactly happened when the gang leader lunged towards me? Stay with me until a bit later in the book. The outcome turned violent, not with me but by the actions of someone else, which takes us down the parallel paths of moral choices and legal rights when coming to the aid of others. This is just as controversial a topic for some as our school's Zero Tolerance approach to defending yourself from bullying, and one I believe is worthy of discussion in its own section in the book.

Self Defense Laws by State (AL - MI)

State	Duty to Retreat	Castle Doctrine	Stand Your Ground Laws
Alabama			X
Alaska			X
Arizona			X
Arkansas	X	X	
California			X
Colorado		X	
Connecticut	X	X	
Delaware	X	X	
Florida			X
Georgia			X
Hawaii	X	X	
Idaho			X
Illinois		X	
Indiana			X
Iowa	X	X	
Kansas			X
Kentucky			X
Louisiana			X
Maine	X	X	
Maryland	X	X	
Massachusetts	X		
Michigan			X
Minnesota	X	X	
Mississippi			X
Missouri			X

Self Defense Laws by State (MO - WY)

State	Duty to Retreat	Castle Doctrine	Stand Your Ground Laws
Montana			X
Nebraska	X	X	
Nevada			X
New Hampshire			X
New Jersey	X	X	
New Mexico*		X	
New York	X	X	
North Carolina			X
North Dakota	X		
Ohio	X		
Oklahoma			X
Oregon*		X	
Pennsylvania			X
Rhode Island	X	X	
South Carolina			X
South Dakota			X
Tennessee			X
Texas			X
Utah			X
Vermont	X		
Virginia*		X	
Washington*		X	
West Virginia			X
Wisconsin		X	
Wyoming			X

*Does not have a specific Castle Doctrine law but provides certain rights within your residence. **Note:** Definitions of Duty to Retreat, or Castle Doctrine laws are subject to change. Consult your local state laws for more information.*

6

COMPARING MARTIAL ARTS & SELF-PROTECTION SYSTEMS

Jennie Finch was an All-American softball pitcher at Arizona, who went on to win an Olympic medal and play professionally. Drafted by the St. Louis Cardinals in 1999, Albert Pujols has been and continues to be a powerful slugger in the Major Leagues. He is a three-time National League Most Valuable Player (MVP) and a ten-time All Star. In the 2004 Pepsi All-Star Softball Game, Finch struck out Pujols. Pujols typically makes some contact with the ball, even those coming in at roughly the 100-mph equivalent speed of Finch's pitches, but in this instance, despite the softball's larger size as compared to a baseball, his swings did not come close. How is it that a hitter as great as Pujols was not able to foul off even one ball?

I believe Finch's release was one reason. Her release point made it effective against batters not used to her style, which was underhand as opposed to baseball's overhand delivery. Her delivery caused the ball to rise. Baseball players, on the other hand, never see a ball tail up, but will instead see balls as coming straight or breaking to the sides or down.

Now take the various styles of martial arts that are out there. All have a unique history, tradition, and beauty, with some incredible displays of physical techniques. Some find their roots in battle, but all have evolved into competition sport. One isn't necessarily any better than the other, just different, with its value subjectively dependent upon a student's goal.

If self-defense is your goal, think about Albert Pujols and how he struck out because he faced an unfamiliar style. What would happen if you were only familiar with one style of fighting and you were suddenly faced with something completely different in a violent encounter?

Your life may very well depend on a must-connect strike executed with sufficient power and precision. That's why I developed my method, Kuaishou (pronounced: Kuai-show) —so we won't have a Finch-Pujols situation. But formal, studio training in Kuaishou is presently limited, and even it was widely available, how would you know if it was any better or worse without some context for comparison? That's why I want to discuss the various disciplines out there so that you'll be able to better choose the right self-protection options for you.

Since I draw from these disciplines, let me again stress my deep appreciation for all of them. I present the following comparisons solely with an eye towards practical and effective self-defense, not on any other criteria, including the many other excellent aspects of these martial art styles and traditions. For simplicity, I've organized the martial arts and self-protection systems discussed into five categories: Kung Fu, Eastern Martial Arts, Southeast Asian Martial Arts, Western Fighting Styles, and Hybrids.

KUNG FU

Kung Fu is an umbrella term for the Chinese martial arts with roots dating back to at least the 5th century BCE. The most popular styles are Wushu, Shaolin, then Wing Chun. There are also well over 400 different sub-styles of Kung Fu that are derived from the "Five Animal" system of Kung Fu schools, usually described as crane, snake, monkey, mantis, tiger, and further sub-styles with names like White Tiger or White Dragon and so on. These systems are very popular in the western part of the United States and usually involve specialized "traditional" weapons, such as the long staff and other weapons that would never be used in modern combat or a street fight. With many of these systems, students wear elaborate costumes and will commonly perform at local events, with the students playing musical instruments and beating drums.

However, Kung Fu systems, outside of Wing Chun, are as ineffective as their Korean and Japanese counterparts. Using too many nerve attacks and having Kung Fu Masters in their 80's knocking out healthy 20-year-olds with their invisible Chi powers has led to numerous videos that make these systems look almost clownish and more like a skit from *Saturday Night Live*. Drawing on thousands of years of wisdom doesn't mean you have the power to wave your hand and stop a 21st century 250-pound man from attacking you.

So, for purposes of comparing martial arts styles useful for practical self-protection, I'm focusing solely on the Wing Chun system of Kung Fu.

Wing Chun

Wing Chun forms the base of my own self-protection system, as I consider it the best close-quarter, traditional, mainstream martial art in the world. I utilize the beneficial aspects of Cantonese-style Wing Chun, as well as certain applications of Chi Sao (pronounced: chee-sow)—also called "sticking hands" used for reflexively responding to an opponent in direct contact. For six years beginning in 1987, I trained under the watchful eye of renowned Sifu (pronounced: see-foo) Tom Wong, who proved to be a huge influence in my life. Wing Chun is a reserved "gentleman's" martial art that makes much use of execution and leverage. With my street fight at Trader Joe's in mind, Wing Chun led to my epiphany: that while tactics are necessary, one also needs to learn about being reserved. Please don't get me wrong. Wing Chun has its share of violence, but I saw early on that Wing Chun would be able to provide me with that mix of violence and discipline that I realized I needed (and we all need) along with some new tools for my arsenal.

Wing Chun emphasizes close-range, quick, linear strikes (strikes that come straight at you) as opposed to hooks. It's efficient—as if your hand is made of metal and it's being attracted to a face or body magnet—with no wasted movement, thus no flamboyance. Unlike many of the disciplines, Wing Chun works well when opponents are six to twelve inches away, which is the distance we most often find ourselves from muggers, aggressors and the like in real-world situations.

But no single traditional martial art system in the world is sufficient for realistic self-defense, which is why I developed my own. All traditional systems teach defenses to counter their own specific type of fighting. Again, think back to the Albert Pujols analogy. With most martial art styles, you are ill-prepared when encountering something outside of that style; you cannot with confidence defend against something you have not been taught to defend against nor practiced.

Wing Chun is no different. Wing Chun's emphasis on linear punches and chain strikes makes it weak against the powerful hooks of a street attack. An attacker who knows how to fight is going to lunge with haymakers and hooks, which are rarely seen in Wing Chun. Wing Chun also provides very little instruction on standing grappling (being grabbed violently, choked, or in a "clinch") and absolutely none on ground fighting (fighting when off your feet). Sorry, but in a street attack, you need to know how to avoid being tackled or clinched, and what to do if—despite your best effort—it happens to you.

PROS

- As a close-range system, the speed of its strikes is a big strength.
- Focus is on simplicity, efficiency, and directness.

- The three main forms of Wing Chun help with stance and arm location.
- The advanced training drills of Chi Sao or "Sticking Hands" effectively improve stance, balance, and "sensitivity" (again though, only in the Wing Chun world of linear attacks and the absence of any grappling).

CONS

- Too much emphasis on linear strikes and the overuse of linear attacks, blocks, and counters weaken Wing Chun. While excellent if you are the one to throw the first punch, it's problematic if you're attempting to defend yourself against something other than a linear strike.
- The forms (movements practiced in the air) are great, but perfecting them takes years, requiring a lot of patience, and they aren't that useful for real-world altercations.
- Not enough attention is given to the application of hook strikes to the head and body, resulting in insufficient attention to blocking these types of strikes.
- There is an absence of any true sparring, a lack of grappling, and even takedowns are very rarely used.
- Most Wing Chun schools offer very little cardio, and you will not find heavy bags or shields, let alone Thai pads or mitts.

- 90% of your time will be spent working on forms that have minimal use in a real fight.
- Anyone who has seen a real fight is hard-pressed to understand the benefits of spending countless hours training on a wooden dummy (called a "mook jong"), an object that does not move nor fight back and yet is a staple of Wing Chun.

EASTERN MARTIAL ARTS

The Eastern martial art systems are comprised of various styles of karate from Japan and Korea. When it comes to traditional Eastern martial arts, the heavy hitters include the Japanese Shotokan, Aikido (the Okinawan version), and Kempo, as well as the Korean systems of Taekwondo (TDK), Goju Ryu, and Hapkido. Most American karate schools are based on the Okinawan systems of Shotokan and Kempo, or the Korean systems of TDK and Goju Ryu. These systems have multiple levels of black belt and have been popularized by Hollywood movies over the last 30 or 40 years.

PROS

- These Eastern systems are good at teaching discipline and commitment, as sports attempt to do in general.
- The Korean schools have perfected welcoming the entire family and believe "the more the merrier" when it comes to class size.

- The Korean schools and Aikido are suited for kids usually from five to ten years old.
- The Japanese schools are usually focused on adults and are a bit more intense...if you like intensity (but nothing like the intensity found in an MMA gym).

CONS

- The plain truth is that there are very few realistic street fighting applications found in all of these systems, *combined*.
- These systems teach how to focus on a singular action and usually teach one technique at a time, like a strike or a kick. While this may seem beneficial for ease of learning, it isn't effective in the real world.
- Most of these martial art schools are built through a pyramid plan of business; if one sticks with training, puts in the time, and goes through the motions, that individual will attain a black belt. One often finds these schools awarding 1st degree black belts to students who are only 7 or 8 years old, or to a 95-year-old who can barely stand.
- With TKD, too many cons exist, especially the jump and spinning kicks, which I find completely ridiculous and are never to be used in a street fight.
- With Shotokan, the waist chambered-based strikes are brutally ineffective, and while the

powerful sidekick associated with this system is pure power, it can rarely be used, except by an expert.

- Aikido is one of the least useful martial arts in the world; the trouble begins in that it has a non-confrontational basis. I find there are far too many wristlocks and flashy rolls. Students literally spend thousands of hours looking at themselves in mirrors and fighting invisible opponents to perfect their numerous forms, or "katas." They gain little realistic fighting abilities through this kind of training.

SOUTHEAST ASIA

Filipino Martial Arts (FMA) evolved in the Philippines and is comprised of three slightly different systems combined to form FMA. These systems are called Arnis, Escrima and Kali, which all have open hand fighting, but they are really known for their incorporation of stick and knife fighting. The FMA's knife trapping and street effectiveness heavily influenced me, so much so that I travelled 40 miles each way to Torrance, California to train with some of the top instructors and students of this system (including Paul Vunak, a talented and interesting character, who started his sessions by taking a massive bong hit!). In the United States, the best known Southeast Asian fighting style is Muay Thai, also known as Thai kickboxing. Originally from Thailand, it spread to a wider region where this fighting style can be found, including Southeast China and Burma (Myanmar). More about Muay Thai follows below. Lastly, from Indonesia we get Pencak Silat, or commonly called "Silat," a much older system than those found in FMA. Although the FMA systems originated in Silat, the Filipinos made the techniques tighter and more kickass.

Muay Thai

Outside of Wing Chun, Muay Thai is the most street effective of any sport martial art and the most effective of any traditional martial art, other than the hybrid systems, such as Krav Maga and Jeet Kune Do (JKD). My own system incorporates Muay Thai's low hook kick to an opponent's lower leg, the 45-degree attacking knee, the upward knee, the elbow strike when used in a standing grapple or clinch, and the hook strike and upper cut.

PROS

- Extremely effective kicks and strikes.
- Violent and more realistic than most martial arts.
- Somewhat easy to learn and very easy to strike hard with intensity.
- Provides the best cardio workout of all the martial arts.
- Provides a good, shared workout, as students, utilizing pads and shields, switch between striking and blocking.
- Imparts a feeling that one is a real fighter when learning this martial art.

CONS

- Most of the knees and elbows must be delivered in a standing grapple position and super close in distance...and this is not street smart.
- The appeal of the hook kick is also its detriment; trained opponents can easily block hook kicks, and hook kicks are usually telegraphed.
- One can easily injure themselves when training, especially if not properly taught how to hold the shields and pads.
- There are few linear threats and the front kicks are usually used to keep your opponent at a distance and not to injure.
- The "live by the sword and die by the sword" commitment to hook kicks, punches, elbows, and knees means that you could be in trouble if you miss as you throw your full self into your kick or strike. In real life, you also may not have as much surrounding space as you need to throw these big, overwhelming kicks and strikes as you do in a Muay Thai ring.

WESTERN MARTIAL ARTS AND HYBRID FIGHTING SYSTEMS

Whereas the Eastern systems are termed the "traditional" martial arts, Western martial art systems are classified as non-traditional. These systems include boxing, kickboxing, wrestling (freestyle), and the newer hybrid systems, such as Krav Maga, Kuaishou, and the Jiu-Jitsu-based Mixed Martial Arts (MMA) businesses. I've included a discussion of Brazilian/Japanese Jiu-Jitsu in this section as well. It's worth noting that Kenpo Karate (not to be confused with Kempo Karate) has its modern roots in Hawaii and became very popular in Southern California—particularly in Pasadena, the Mecca for American Karate. Ed Parker started Kenpo, and the first karate club in America was at Caltech in 1957, just before Parker started his system in the 1960's.

Many aspects of these Western systems are extremely beneficial, with more of a focus on cardio and sparring. Training in the hybrid systems raises the heartbeat more than the Eastern systems. Outside of Krav Maga and Jiu-Jitsu, there is no belt system, which is both good and bad.

PROS

- Boxing, kickboxing, and wrestling provide an intense cardio workout, and this is what some people truly need (and enjoy) to get into—and stay in—shape.
- Boxing is perhaps the best system of basic self-defense. It teaches striking and countering in a realistic fashion, and the sparring will provide improved confidence in the event of a real confrontation. Boxing best prepares an individual for a street fight; it provides the best instruction

on how to protect oneself, and its strikes are even quicker than those in Wing Chun.

- I consider Krav Maga the most realistic of all the mainstream martial art systems. Its quick strikes and kicks will take down most opponents, and the techniques taught for disarming a knife-wielding attacker are very useful.

- Others consider MMA as the cream of the crop when it comes to realistic self-defense. Along with some stand up striking, students are taught how to grapple and ground fight (whereas boxing and kickboxing have no ground training at all and Krav Maga has very little to offer). MMA sparring —with its heavy focus and mix on ground fighting, takedowns, and boxing—utilizes both stand up and groundwork, which was not found in any mainstream martial art until MMA took hold 15-20 years ago.

CONS

- Boxing offers no grappling or ground fighting, and there are no kicks, knees, or elbows used.
- Rampant injuries are prevalent in MMA schools. I'm not talking just the bumps and bruises that you'll find with boxing and wrestling, but serious injuries, such as fractures and every type of knee injury you see in professional football.
- Both MMA schools and boxing gyms have too much sparring. The human body is not meant for

such heavy sparring, especially given what we now know about head injuries and the brutal consequences of concussions.

- MMA schools and competition-based fighting systems focus on anger and train to increase an individual's hostility. This mindset for competitive battle is essential, but it must be taught in conjunction with controlling one's anger and not wearing it on one's sleeve. Nowadays, most MMA students are in their twenties and sport tattoos instead of belts or trophies.

- Krav Maga is a product of the Israeli military and instills a militant mindset. I find it difficult to justify the use of a combat system designed to kill or maim for most street fights or general self-defense scenarios.

Jiu-Jitsu

Not to the extent of Muay Thai, but I also utilize some techniques from the martial art Jiu-Jitsu (also spelled "Ju Jitsu") in my methodology. There is Japanese and Brazilian Jiu-Jitsu, and they are extremely similar...even though the Brazilian boys may not agree with me. Brazilian Jiu-Jitsu rose to prominence about 20 years ago mainly, in my opinion, because of its ground fighting. I believe that ground fighting is essential to an overall fight plan, and for decades the popular Japanese and Korean martial arts (including Wing Chun and other Chinese Kung Fu systems) avoided any groundwork, instead teaching ridiculous and ineffective anti-grappling techniques.

PROS

- Ground fighting, again which I believe to be essential, is very easy to learn and is a system one can become proficient at in a reasonably short time (less than a year).
- Ground fighting is easier because one spends 95-99% of the time on the mat, usually in a guard or mounted position.
- People who are usually weaker at sports or athletics like grappling because of its ease with smaller students, who usually do very well; smaller individuals who have avoided sports or martial arts really seem to take to grappling.
- Reverse chokeholds and guard positions are extremely relevant to realistic fighting systems and can be used in most street fights.

CONS

- One could be knocked out in ground fighting against multiple opponents.
- The asphalt and concrete composition of the ground hurts in a street fight, compared to the three-inch cushion mats used by all grappling studios.

- Jiu-Jitsu's ground-based fascination has led to the belief that all fights should end with some type of choke or arm bar...and this is far from the truth.
- While Jiu-Jitsu is very good for cage fighting, it is extremely dangerous for any street fight because, especially in street fighting, you never want to be on your back or on your knees. You need to stay on your feet, using side mounts or back (rear) positions only when you know you're facing a single attacker, and holding or controlling them until the police arrive.

Kuaishou

In developing Kuaishou, I took Bruce Lee's lead, "take what is useful, and discard what is useless." I derived the system, a contemporary martial art, from a unique combination of fighting styles...primarily Western boxing, traditional far-Eastern martial arts, and my own techniques designed to increase overall speed, kinetic strength, and explosive energy. The explosive nature of the proactive attack comes from the athletic moves used in football (integrated from my experience as a fullback and a linebacker at USC), and other contact sports, where quick, powerful, lower body energy is used not just to move to, but to "move through" your opponent.

Beyond the *"Inside"* awareness elements already discussed, Kuaishou (Cantonese for "fast hands") emphasizes a practical and highly effective form of personal defense. It incorporates and blends original techniques with techniques from other combat arts, and it differs from martial arts that have evolved into modern-day competition sports, namely Judo, Karate, Muay Thai, Jiu-jitsu, boxing, and mixed martial arts fighting. As mentioned before, in these other disciplines, opponents of similar styles compete in a controlled setting with set rules. In contrast, Kuaishou is designed to counter violence in real-life, uncontrolled situations. This hybrid fighting system emphasizes proactive attacking when faced with a potentially violent threat and using surprise, speed, and overwhelming fury as an advantage for the person under threat, regardless of size or strength. A Kuaishou fight, by design, is intended to end a violent confrontation in seconds. When you may need to fight for your life, you don't want a sport...you want what will work and work fast.

PROS

- Singularly designed for self-protection. Realistic, using default attacking and defensive moves for beginners that are easy to learn and remember, as well as advanced training in weapons defense and control of opponents.
- Uses a blend of boxing, martial arts, and proprietary techniques to deploy in close quarters and against skilled or unskilled opponents.
- Emphasizes proper mindset and proactive techniques, taking advantage of surprise and speed, especially useful against bigger, stronger assailants.
- Integrates micro sparring into training to safely

develop hand speed, hand-eye and foot coordination, and intensity.

CONS

- Limited availability of certified instructors outside of Southern California.
- Not suited for students interested in martial art competitions.
- Not designed for or offered to younger children and preteens.
- Doesn't offer the rich traditions, uniforms, or pageantry of the more traditional martial arts.

Exploring Your Options

After all I've written, I realize that unless you live in Southern California, you can't physically take my Kuaishou training (at least, not yet), and the other disciplines currently remain your only options. That's OK. I wanted to include my system into the comparison so that—if you feel it's a system suited for you—then you can search your own local area for studios emphasizing some of the same principles and techniques. I highly recommend that everyone learn at least some self-defense training. I'm not suggesting that a two-hour seminar is sufficient, but it needn't take two years either.

Here are some guidelines you may wish to use:

• Don't pigeonhole yourself into just one category. Look for a facility that teaches hybrid disciplines and incorporates both stand up and ground fighting.

• Search for a proactive system. Most systems are truly based on reactive self-defense, where one reacts only when attacked first. You don't want to be in a position of having to react, losing the advantages of surprise and speed. Rather than being reactionary, you want to learn how to initiate the attack and effectively neutralize your opponent before he tries to hurt you.

• Consider the practical application of the style of self-protection you are evaluating. Will you be able to use what is being offered to defend yourself in real-life situations, such as an intruder in your house, or is it simply about choreographed routines and perhaps a good aerobic workout? For example, while they might look nice, high jump kicks won't do the trick. Unless you're an expert, you're bound to miss altogether, fall, and get your butt whipped.

Training Time

Ask questions: For instance, how often will you be training? I consider the perfect amount of training to be twice a week for an hour to an hour-and-a-half per session. Beyond that, you're really putting too much into your training. For this amount of training, you should expect to pay $150-$200 per month (if paying for a child, it should be under $100 month-ly). You should be able to pay on a month-to-month basis with the ability to cancel with reasonable notice at any time.

Group Size

Find out about the group size. I don't recommend private training exclusively. An instructor cannot fully observe a student in a one-on-one situation. The best way to learn a system is to participate in a small class of ideally six to ten students. Private training on top of that is more effective, if desired. That said, you'd usually find a typical class size is about eight to twelve students. I would hesitate to join a class of 18 or more unless we are talking about a child; with chil-dren, larger classes create energy. And with younger kids, ensure that they're training with children their own age.

Inquire as to whether different levels of expertise are offered. Your goal should be to move up those levels to obtain advanced skills, not just to obtain a belt or rank. Even with different levels of expertise offered, with twice-weekly train-ing, you should be able to proficiently use the techniques you are being taught within 8 to 12 months.

Kids

For kids, the focus should be on more of a sport martial art (if anything, it's the parents, not the kids, who should be concentrating on a life or death self-defense system, such as Kuaishou or Krav Maga). For children younger than ten, assuming you have options in your community, Karate and

Tae Kwon Do are tailor-made. Both disciplines will teach young children focus, discipline, athleticism, balance, stretching, and respect.

Regarding respect, the respect taught does not just relate to a respect for the teacher and the discipline, but also a respect for others; seniority is based on the amount of time an individual has studied a discipline, not on age, so it's not uncommon to find older children bowing to younger ones in true respect.

As for focus, I've seen kids as young as five years old gain tremendous focus from martial arts (and their parents tell me these kids carry this same focus with them into other pursuits, like their school work). For instance, where other kids were aimlessly wandering around the outfield picking weeds, one young child's focus enabled him to excel as a pitcher (as well as to become a state chess champion), and his parents attributed his focus to the martial arts training that he received starting at age five. For ages 10-12, I think the introduction of some ground fighting and grappling is beneficial (younger than 10, the kids just end up wrestling, not grappling). So, for these older kids, I would augment the training with Judo or Jiu-Jitsu. At this age, the kids are also old enough to learn boxing and kickboxing.

Competitive martial arts for kids are best, in my opinion, for children over the age of 10. Competition starting at this age is beneficial for teaching the relationship between hard work (training) and success, but should also be fun. The time commitment can be demanding, however, and it can be expensive.

Management & Operations

What does your gut instinct tell you about the Sensei (pronounced: sen-say) or Sifu or whatever they may call their
instructors? (Sensei means "teacher," and the Sifu is usually
a master teacher or instructor, or spiritual leader—often the
owner of the studio or dojo). Is it someone you or your child
will be able to learn from, or do they seem to be driven by
some sort of ego thing? You want someone who will instill
self-assurance, not someone trying to create intensity or
present an overt machismo. I have found that reserved individuals—those who exude quiet confidence—typically make
the best instructors when it comes to teaching the reserved
aggression needed in these various disciplines.

Cleanliness is extremely important, especially in a grappling school, like Judo or Jiu-Jitsu. You have a greater chance
to catch skin infections, ringworm, and even common colds
if the mats aren't cleaned with bleach daily. Inquire!

Martial art schools use a variety of training equipment.
Make sure that it has the basics. A traditional Karate or Tae
Kwon Do school should have a thin padded floor, usually
with a mirrored wall and perhaps some striking shields. A
Kung Fu school will usually have a hardwood floor with
minimal shields or other padded equipment. You'll also find
a wooden floor in a Wing Chun school, along with a wooden
dummy or mook jong. A Jiu-Jitsu school will have a thicker,
padded floor (for ground fighting, throws, and takedowns)
and few, if any, shields or pads for striking. The newer MMA
schools will have flooring much like a Jiu-Jitsu school, but
they will also have shields and pads for kicking and striking.

MMA schools will also have heavy bags (like you see in a boxing gym) as well as the longer banana bags; these are twice as long and twice as heavy and used for practicing low kicks. A person who really wants to learn realistic self-defense should look into a school that offers a variety of techniques that are suited for uncontrolled violent encounters, and where they can be reasonably proficient in a matter of months, not years.

Comparison of Martial Arts and Self-Protection Systems

SYSTEM	ORIGIN	PRACTICAL FOR SELF PROTECTION	INJURY RISK IN TRAINING	KID FRIENDLY (under 12)	LAW ENFORCE-MENT UTILITY	CARDIO BENEFIT	COMPETITION FOCUSED
KUNG FU							
Wing Chun	Chinese	Moderate	Low	No	Limited	Limited	No
Shoulin	Chinese	Low	Low	No	Limited	Limited	No
Wushu	Chinese	Low	Low	Yes	Limited	Limited	No
EASTERN MARTIAL ARTS							
Shotokon Karate	Japanese	Moderate	Low	Yes	Limited	Limited	Yes
Aikido	Japanese	Limited	Low	Yes	Limited	Limited	No
Jiu-jitsu/Judo	Japanese	Limited	Low	Yes	Limited	Limited	Yes
Goju Ryu	Japanese	Moderate	Low	Yes	Limited	Limited	Yes
Kempo Karate	Japanese	Moderate	Low	Yes	Limited	Limited	Yes
Taekwondo (TKD)	Korean	Limited	Low	Yes	Limited	Limited	Yes
Hapkido	Korean	Limited	Low	No	Limited	Limited	Yes
WESTERN							
Boxing	Europe/USA	High	Moderate	No	High	High	Yes
Wrestling- Freestyle	Ancient Greece	Limited	Low	Yes	Limited	High	Yes
Kenpo Karate	USA	Moderate	Low	No	Moderate	Moderate	No
HYBRIDS							
Krav Maga	Israeli	High	High	No	High	Limited	No
Kickboxing	Filipino/USA	Moderate	High	No	Moderate	High	No
Kuaishou	USA/Chinese	High	Low	No	High	Moderate	No
MMA/BJJ	Brazil/Japan/USA	High	High	No	Moderate	High	Yes
JKD	USA/Chinese	High	Moderate	No	Moderate	Moderate	No
SOUTHEAST ASIA							
Kali	Filipino	Moderate	Low	No	Limited	Low	No
Escrema	Filipino	Moderate	Low	No	Limited	Low	No
Pencat Salat	Indonesian	Moderate	Low	No	Limited	Low	No
Muay Thai	Thailand	Moderate	High	No	Limited	High	Yes

7

TECHNIQUES TO DELIVER PAIN, DEFEND, OR ESCAPE

If you have any doubts that a much smaller and untrained person can effectively deliver debilitating pain to a much larger man, I can attest to the fact that one of the most excruciatingly painful experiences of my entire life was inflicted on me by a 17-pound infant named Adam, my youngest son! Both of us were crawling around on the floor trying to cobble together an architectural masterpiece with Tinkertoys. When I made a quick turn to show baby Adam the critical connecting piece we'd been searching for, I was met with a 4-inch wooden dowel into my right cornea. I'm sure at 12 months old he didn't do it on purpose, but he did send me an early warning that his father, a Kung Fu master no less, could be defeated, easily, and without a single lesson in weapons or personal defense. I had never experienced something so painful in my life. Stunned, I rolled up on both knees for several minutes, pressing the palm of my hand over my eye, which was gushing with tears. Eventually, my head sank into both hands, and I remember thinking, *Somebody, please put me out of my misery! They shoot horses, don't they?*

Five years later, I was training martial arts from a makeshift studio in my garage. I had a heavy bag, some mitts and protective gear, and a few sticks (batons) for weapons training. Suddenly, and without warning, I was whacked from behind, right across my kidneys. I immediately dropped to the ground and felt a rolling shockwave through my entire body. It was indescribably painful—as bad as the eye jab with the Tinker toy—but different in its form of agony, and not nearly as creative. When I rolled over to see what freight train had jumped the tracks and slammed into me, there he was again, my son Adam, now age six, holding one of my practice batons with an astonished look on his face that seemed to quietly mumble "I can't believe I got him again. Sucker!"

The point to my two stories is obvious: either my son has had it out for me since infancy, or—what I choose to believe is the real lesson—small people, even tiny people, can bring on tremendous pain to very big and strong people, either by luck, by accident, or by proper technique. Surviving a violent encounter by luck or by accident is great—if it happens—but it probably won't be enough for most of us. So, let's look at a limited, but very effective selection, of self-protection techniques.

You can learn and practice these techniques on your own, but it's always helpful to have a training partner—a Kung Fu buddy to help you—like a friend or family member to alternate with as aggressor or defender. To assist in your understanding, you'll find some demonstrative photos accompanying each of these techniques, as well as a link to our website where you'll find videos for each technique fully executed (www.defensekinetics.com/videos). Start out mimicking the foot and handwork slowly...very slowly. Then gradually increase your speed as you gain precision and fluidity. Be certain you are in control of your movements to prevent injuring your practice partner or yourself, and never use force on any unprotected part of the head or body. Remember, it doesn't take much to deliver serious pain or even injury to someone, especially if they are unprotected and unprepared. Heavy bags and practice dummies at your local gym, sporting goods store, or self-defense studio are designed to take brute force strikes, or even chokes and kicks, but not your little brother!

The purpose of the techniques you're going to read about is to inflict pain. In my opinion, pain infliction is the appropriate response to any real or perceived act of aggression. Moderate to severe pain will stun your assailant and either end his aggression or provide you with enough time to escape. The more severe the pain, the more compliant the assailant will be, either because he can no longer tolerate it, or because the viciousness of his attack required you to respond with enough force to cause injuries that impaired his ability to continue his attack. In other words, you broke his collarbone.

Yes, people have written books and preached about the use of brutal means to put down violent threats—and I have no qualms about taking someone's life who is trying to take mine (or anyone that I choose to protect), but it is exceptionally rare that something this extreme is called for. This book is not about the ramifications of taking someone else's life, especially when pain infliction is a measured response in almost all cases of violent threats. And in the infliction of pain, contrary to killing someone, these techniques aren't designed to produce life-threatening consequences. In fact, with most of these techniques, the effects are short-lived. That said, any physical contact with another person could lead to unintended consequences. A punch to the jawline, or a simple push, can cause a person to lose control and fatally slam their head or neck onto a concrete sidewalk. A Brachial Stun delivered to a person with a heart problem could lead to cardiac arrest. There's always some risk of creating more injury than intended, which is a lot easier to justify in a real-life violent encounter, but not with a practice partner! Go slow and be certain of your control before increasing the tempo.

So just what are these pain-inflicting techniques? I'm going to break them down into four categories:

- Body shots
- Head and neck strikes
- Eye jabs
- Chokes

*Neutral Stance. This is your "ready" position: poised to attack or defend,
yet non-confrontational.*

I'll also teach you some basic *defense* defaults, including blocks, choke escapes, and countering maneuvers. No matter the technique though, you want to make sure that you aren't telegraphing it in advance of its execution. The best way to do this is to start with a neutral stance, feet apart, lining up just outside of your shoulders. Place your natural or dominant leg slightly in front of the other, where the opposite toe is directly across from the heel of your leading foot. Place both hands in front of your chest, palms mostly toward the threat, as if pleading or negotiating. This "neutral" or "ready stance" serves two important purposes: it conveys to the other person a non-threatening posture (as opposed to two clinched and raised fists, one in front of the other), while setting yourself up to respond quickly with an attack or to defend yourself against an incoming punch.

Whenever possible, all strikes should be executed from this neutral position. If you begin your strike with your hands down by your side, you're wasting precious time to defend or strike. You're also more apt to telegraph your intentions with an obvious upward shoulder movement, or do some sort of needless windup to your punch, providing your opponent with plenty of advanced notice of what's about to come.

BODY SHOTS

Body shots or blows are the best choice for causing pain and putting an assailant down. It is my preferred area of attack because several parts of the body are vulnerable, easy to strike, (as opposed to a smaller moving target like the head), and the pain inflicted ranges from moderate to severe depending on which part of the body you strike. Also, there are very few instances when you can't execute a body shot. Further, because an assailant will typically be looking at your facial area, a body shot occurs out of their direct line of site, unlike an incoming shot to their head, which enters their field of view and can result in having it blocked or dodged by ducking. Finally, with untrained fighters, body shots are rarely anticipated, making them even harder to block! Instinctually, you'll want to go for a shot to the head...but don't do it! Go for the body, if possible.

To illustrate my conviction, look at boxing champion Vasiliy Lomachenko's 2018 fight with Jorge Linares.

Lomachenko put Linares on his knees with a technical knockout (or TKO) in the 10th round, ending the fight with a body shot. Interestingly, earlier, in the sixth round, Lomachenko survived a brutal right-hand strike from Linares directly to the face. It knocked the legs right out from under the Ukrainian fighter, but it wasn't enough to stop him (nor did it cut him or cause his nose to bleed). The shot that ended the fight was a left hook, perfectly placed on Jorge Linares's liver.

With our body shots, you'll generally be aiming for the centerline. By striking here, you are directly attacking the body's central nervous system. The core parts of the body within this target zone—the heart, lungs, liver and kidneys—all lay directly to the immediate left or right of this centerline. I'm going to discuss four places around the centerline where strikes prove particularly effective:

- The liver
- The solar plexus/diaphragm
- The ribs
- The belly

These areas are all extremely vulnerable, so it's easy to inflict excruciating pain, to knock the wind out of an opponent, or to deteriorate his ability to effectively fight back. In doing so, the adage "destroy the body and the head will die" readily applies.

The Liver Shot

Far and away, if you only learn one strike, this is it. Striking the liver of your assailant will cause him to be in excruciating pain immediately. This shot will put your assailant on the ground in total agony and leave him in an uncommunicative heap where he will not be able to stand for up to 4-5 minutes (and it can easily render him unconscious for the first minute).

Left-handed liver strike using a three-quarter closed fist.

Why is this strike so intense and debilitating? The liver, being the largest organ in the abdomen, is encapsulated by the most nerve fibers (and it's also partially unprotected by the rib cage, further making it the ideal target). When struck, the nerve fibers deform and send a shock wave to the brain. The result is that the blood pressure completely crashes, the pupils dilate, and all control of bodily functions is lost.

Increase power using the Drive Strike to the left with a horizontal right fist to the liver (can also be used to the belly, ribs, or solar-plexus).

The excruciating, stabbing pain, along with a feeling of full paralysis, results in the assailant collapsing to the ground in a fetal position, unable to move and just trying to survive. In fact, his brain intentionally directs him to the ground in a last-ditch attempt to get more blood to it. The pain is so intense that it can, as stated before, result in fainting or unconsciousness.

How effective is this blow? Let me put it this way, Lomachenko and many other champion fighters have used a good liver shot to end fights. If you can deliver an effective shot to the liver, you'll have just taught your assailant a powerful lesson: pain overrides all their criminal intent. The intense vigor they used to try and intimidate you disappears into a world of agony that they cannot control.

As for the actual strike, you'll be aiming for an assailant's liver in what will be—for you, the striker—the upper left of the assailant's abdomen. You will have a direct shot at it with your left-hand (I recommend using a horizontal closed fist turned 45 degrees to the right).

However, most of us are right-handed and many people won't feel comfortable using their non-dominant hand for a first strike. If you're one of these people, I suggest using what I call a "Drive Strike." Here, you turn your right hand over for a closed-fisted, horizontal punch. This all starts with a big step using your left leg just to the left side of your opponent. Your right fist quickly follows. Then, as if finishing a baseball pitch, drive your right fist into his liver.

The Solar Plexus/Diaphragm Shot

Simply put, hitting someone in their solar plexus causes their diaphragm to spasm. The target area is just below the sternum and above the belly button. The assailant will drop straight to the ground with the wind knocked out of them.

They'll be gasping for air and in severe pain for up to about 30 seconds (beware, they may also vomit).

To deliver this shot, use a closed-fist punch with a linear step (straight between the opponent's legs), where your fist is turned vertically—so the thumb is directly on top.

An attack step forward with a vertical fist to the solar plexus is lightning fast and extremely difficult to block.

Depending on the opponent's height, it's (more or less) a straight extension of your elbow directly into the solar plexus. And a good rule of thumb for this (or any strikes, including those where you use weapons) is you'd rather hit too low than too high. This is a classic Wing Chun-style strike to the solar plexus, achieved by forcefully stepping deep and directly between the assailant's feet. (If you're right-handed, step deep with your right leg. If left-handed, step deep with your left leg). Your striking hand is on the same side as your stepping leg. Lower your weight while stepping in to add more power to your punch and to dodge any incoming strike.

At impact, your head should be just above your striking fist. I like to use my opposite hand (positioned close to my ear) to block any lucky punch that slips in, and to quickly deliver a second shot to the ribs, liver, or belly. As with most of my techniques, maximum effectiveness comes from surprise, speed, and forward energy. Be careful not to tele-graph your strike by lifting your shoulder or by moving your elbow backward before moving forward. These are common mistakes, and it takes a bit of practice to eliminate these bad habits from your form. Think of your elbow as being a piece of lead placed directly in front of a powerful magnet, moving forward with tremendous speed in a straight line to the target. Keep your elbows by your sides, touching your body to prevent flaring them out; a flaring elbow (an elbow moving away from the body before moving forward) causes a loss of speed and power, and it may signal your intent to strike in advance. And using a vertical strike into your opponent puts into practice the old rule that the quickest way from Point A to Point B is a straight line. This makes it almost impossible for the intended target to block it in time.

Lastly, I can't emphasize enough the importance of forward energy in your attack. It's something I learned to appreciate as a college football linebacker. At 5'11" and 235 pounds, I was considered an undersized player, especially at a football program like the University of Southern California, where every offensive lineman in the late 1980's and early 1990's was between 285 and 300 pounds. I learned then how crucial it was for me to stay low and attack with more ferocity than the giant guy opposing me, who was hell-bent on leveling me on the field.

And it's every bit as crucial in fighting too. It doesn't come naturally to most people, however, and with good reason. After all, most of us instinctively don't want to be near a person who's threatening us; we want to be further away. We don't want to get hit by his fists, or kicked, so we maintain a distance and try to "reach in" with a punch while keeping our head back. The problem is that you'll lose all or most of your forward energy. It may sound counterintuitive, but the technique that I teach is to step deeper than you ever thought you would toward your attacker, placing yourself in the exact area he is occupying. Not only does this completely surprise an assailant, your forward energy takes away his balance, and your proximity either causes his punches to swing past your head, or leaves him no room to throw an effective body shot. Meanwhile, the forward energy behind your strikes makes them powerful and overwhelming, and causes your target to lose their balance and become disoriented. Fight over.

A woman fighting off a bigger man especially needs the advantage of the extra power that forward energy adds to your strikes. A well-placed shot to the solar plexus will usually drop a grown man to the ground. Even if one or two of your punches don't immediately knock him down, your opponent is likely to be hunched forward and off-balance. This gives you the opportunity to deliver several more blows during his attempt to regain his footing or reposition himself to face you. During your flurry of strikes, if he instinctively reaches to his gut for protection, go for the open head. If he covers his head, go for the body. Be opportunistic.

The Rib Shot

I love ribs! I love barbecuing them slathered in sauce, and I love busting them on my opponent if he messes with me, or my baby back ribs. The rib shot is one of only two shots that I discuss in this chapter that will result in a lasting effect, and it will bring agony to the bad guy for weeks. Ribs are like the clavicle (collarbone) in that they're just as crunchy and easy to break. We all come with ribs on both sides of the body, but the easiest and best to bust up are the floating ribs, the ribs at the bottom of the rib cage and not attached directly to the breastbone. These ribs are like a dartboard and your fists are the darts piercing into the body. Any ribs just below the chest are the bullseye. If you're throwing a left, aim a tad lower and further left than the liver shot. Step into your opponent with the left leg and drive your punch into his lower ribs with a closed fist at a 45-degree angle or a horizontal strike (fist parallel to the ground, knuckles up). Again, always think of driving your punch four to six inches into the target. This will ensure you bring enough power into your strike instead of "tapping" the target, which does nothing.

Rib shot using a right side step with a 45 degree closed fist.

You can also use the Drive Strike to attack the ribs. It's the same Drive Step I discussed above with the liver shot, where you step with your left leg to the outside left of your opponent and use your right fist to slam into his ribs, or step your right leg to the outside right of your opponent and using your left fist to strike. Drop your weight down and forward as you drive into your opponent. Take a deeper step than you think you'll need. Your head will drop to his chest level, but keep your eyes and chin up. Never look straight down at the ground. You'll want to keep a good field of vision to see what's going on and what may be coming next. If you landed solidly into his ribs, chances are nothing is coming next except his collapse and moan.

If you want to speed up the delivery of your shot to the ribs, and if you have a chance to practice, you can use the lightning fast "Wing Chun" technique; it's the opposite of the Drive Strike and of western boxing. Here, if you're throwing with your right, have your right hand in the lead (or forward) position in front of your chest. Step into the strike with your right leg. You can either step deep between the legs of your opponent or step just outside of his right leg. Either way, aiming at the ribs, your strike will have a natural hook to it, causing your elbow to slightly flare out from your body. That's OK; with this strike, your opponent will only see your head coming straight at him, not your rib shot. If you throw the punch with your left hand, step into your opponent with your left leg. You can increase the power of this hook punch by lowering your weight as you step, turning your hips quickly in sync and in the same direction as the strike. Your fist can be in a 45-degree or horizontal position. The quicker you turn your hips, the more horizontal your fist will become and the more powerful your blow. The floating ribs will be just above your opponent's hipbone (which is hard as a rock and something you don't want to hit). This shot is an exception to the rule "when in doubt, hit lower than higher."

The Belly Shot

The belly is the largest area on the body to strike, and belly fat does not fully protect the target from the force of a properly executed strike. You cannot miss with a striking area that on average offers up to at least a square foot of landing area. Here again, you can attack the belly with a variety of strikes using either your left or right fist. In the Wing Chun Strike (right leg leads and the right fist strikes, assuming you are right-handed), you use the same closed-fist linear strike employed in the solar plexus shot, except this time your aim is lower. You want to aim at the belly button, but you don't need to be that accurate with this shot to knock the wind out of an assailant and put him on the ground for at least a minute.

Belly shots are also under the direct eye line of your attacker, making them more difficult to block in time. Step in deep between your opponent's legs, lowering your weight, and strike as if you're trying to penetrate five inches deep into his belly. Alternately, you can step toward your opponent with your left leg and deliver the strike with your right fist, the more traditional boxing lead hand for right-handers. This belly shot has all the factors that create power, using the forward driving motion of our step which in turns uses our weight along with the turning the hips in sync with the shoulders for maximum power.

Belly shot thrown from a left side Drive Strike with a vertical fist.

Lastly, you can use the Drive Strike to attack the belly with tremendous force. It's the same Drive Strike explained previously, and you can use a vertical or horizontal fist to land the punch. The Drive Strike uses a big step to the side of your assailant which not only delivers power with the punch, but sets you up beautifully to the outside of your opponent, forcing him to reface (turn toward you) to protect or counter strike, and in that time, you should have already delivered at least two more shots. The belly shot is easy to execute, hard to defend, and highly effective. It's the trifecta of body blows! Trust your fist and let it fly...and bury your fist deep into your assailant's belly.

What about a belly shot to someone with an oversized mid-section? This is often a matter of debate. Under that cushion of fat could be a tremendous amount of muscle—essentially a strong, fat guy. My suggestion: the liver, solar plexus, and ribs are equally as exposed on a larger bellied person, so target these areas first. However, be sure to protect yourself; a heavy guy will have more power in his punches, even if he looks out of shape, and he'll be faster on his feet than you'd expect, at least initially, until he quickly tires out. In any event, stay off the ground, where his weight would be a huge advantage.

Attacking Forearm

The Attacking Forearm is a relatively easy and very effective method for getting an assailant away from you, or to unleash intense and brutal force against him. The forearm used in conjunction with a big attack step will launch anyone backward with more force than you ever thought possible. It also keeps you low, giving you the leverage of a low attack angle needed to put down a much larger person. Whether you need to create some space between you and your opponent (to more effectively strike or kick), halt an incoming hail of flying fists, or knock back your attacker to allow you to escape, the Attacking Forearm is another "go-to" default self-protection technique that I teach my students to practice and perfect.

The Attacking Forearm uses your forearm (the ulna) as the leading edge of your "weapon" while using your body's forward energy to drive an opponent back. Attacking low (to the belly) drops the assailant straight down, while attacking higher (to the chest) can send the opponent flying back 10-20 feet. It's that powerful!

The Attacking Forearm is especially effective for women or smaller persons to drive larger assailants back.

If I were to use a full-speed Attacking Forearm against someone, they would easily go through the wall in any modern house or office. It's also the most effective way to attack someone from the side or from behind if the goal is to knock them out by slamming them into any nearby wall.

One reason this technique is so effective is that nobody expects it! Who comes charging straight at you when you should be cowering in fear? The attack requires you to lower your weight (your head is about the same level as your opponent's chest) and place your dominant forearm across your chest, with your other hand directly behind it (in the "ready" position).

The Attacking Forearm uses an explosive attack step directly into the assailant and a slight upward thrust of the forearm.

In effect, you're making a "t" shape with your right forearm and left hand, or vice versa. Now, drop your weight and lunge toward your attacker's body, leading with your dominant leg and pushing off with your trailing leg. Drive directly into your opponent, applying a slight upward angle on contact. The trailing hand doesn't make contact; it merely stays in position to assist with balance and to be ready to use to strike or block. I've knocked people out the door and into a busy street with a single Attacking Forearm, so be careful how you use it if the situation isn't life or death. This is also a great technique to use if the attack comes to you by surprise, or if you're taking on a flurry of punches and need to get your attacker off and away from you. More details on using this technique as a defensive move or counter attack are explained later.

Final Note on Body Shots

You may be wondering why I didn't roll out the red carpet for strikes to the groin area. After all, it seems to be the "go-to" strike taught to women in self-defense seminars all over America, and if you've experienced or watched athletes double over from such a shot, you know how painful a hit to the groin can be. But, perhaps you've also noticed that you don't often see this happening. That's because the groin area is not as big as you think it is, it calls for a lower shot, and even then, you must strike it the right way to avoid the thigh receiving the brunt of the strike; a thigh strike will do almost nothing. Moreover, for as much pain as a groin strike can deliver, an adrenaline-infused attacker can often continue through the groin strike, perhaps doubling over in agony after the altercation. If it's the only target open, take it. Otherwise, with much better options available, in most cases, I would not recommend a groin strike be your first strike.

HEAD AND NECK STRIKES

It isn't about blood or knocking teeth out. It's about pain because pain overrides EVERYTHING! Again, our first instinct is to throw a fist punch at the head—which is a bad idea. The head is the hardest part of the human body. You will cause very little damage to your assailant and more importantly, you will only inflict moderate pain to him and perhaps even greater pain to you. It's very common for people to injure their hands with blows to the head, usually resulting in a fracture or break of the pinky finger area of the hand where the neck of the metacarpal bone is located. This joint is so highly prone to injury in a closed-fist activity that orthopedic surgeons and professional fighters commonly refer to the injury as a "boxer's break." Your surprise punch will probably result in you breaking—if not crushing—your hand (and needing multiple surgeries to repair it), and you'll be facing one very angry assailant. Further, a punch to the mouth isn't all that painful, and may cause your opponent's teeth to lodge into your fist, along with a blood-to-blood bodily fluid exchange with your criminal attacker...again, with little pain infliction. How many times have you seen an NHL hockey player have some teeth knocked out and yet they stay in the game with very little pain after the initial trauma? Finally, if you're small and your assailant is tall (creating a real height differential between you and the assailant), your stretch will cause you to have less power with a head shot than a body shot.

So why bother to learn about shots to the head or neck? The simple answer is: because the body may be properly guarded with no clean shot available. Your opponent's hands and elbows are low, and he may be tucked over low at the waist, making his body a smaller target. If he's guarding low, we go upstairs, where his hands aren't, temporarily short-circuiting his computer (his brain), and bringing on significant pain if you're targeting the right areas. Head and neck shots are also preferable for fights in very confined spaces. Be it a shot to the head or neck, the strike is executed the exact same way, and the techniques you'll learn here aren't punches, but open-hand strikes to improve accuracy and prevent injury to your hand. Moreover, when you strike with an open hand, you naturally stay more relaxed and can strike with much more speed than with a fist, where people tend to tense their body when delivering the strike. Open-hand strikes are very powerful, yet they get little respect. The fact is, the more joints you eliminate during the delivery of a strike, the stronger the strike becomes because joints bend and fracture much easier than solid bone. These are the reasons why, as a general rule of thumb, I advise students to use a closed fist on the body and open-palm strikes for above the shoulders. We teach both of course, but it takes considerable training to throw effective, accurate, and powerful closed-fist punches to the head without injuring yourself in the process.

Ear Whip

The Ear Whip is my go-to head shot. You can learn to properly execute this strike with just a bit of practice, and it is devastatingly effective. There are two ways to step into this headshot, but for beginners, it's usually easier and more powerful to use the Drive Strike step to your attacker's opposite side, as described earlier. If you are right-handed, step with your left foot to the left of your opponent, landing just outside his foot. As you initiate your Drive Step, with an open palm, extend your elbow about a foot to the right of your attacker's head, leaving a slight, upward bend at the elbow. The moment your left foot hits the ground, quickly snap your hips to the left and use your right shoulder to initiate a whipping action down your right arm. Aim the heel of your open palm toward the back of his ear (you'll end up striking the ear). The powerful strike to the ear, temple, and jawline area of the side of the head is where the carotid sinus is located, and it will drop most men instantly to the ground. It's as painful as it is discombobulating, (and even if you miss the ear, you're likely to shock the nerves surrounding the jawline and carotid sinus sufficiently to do the job).

*The Ear Whip uses the heel of your open palm in a whipping action
capable of a knockout shot.*

The Ear Whip is <u>not a slap</u>. Slapping your attacker will only anger them and delivers no useful pain. The key to this headshot is the power of the whipping action and the force of the heel of your palm and upper wrist into or near the ear. Your open palm starts the whip action about 12 inches from the ear, and then the forward energy from your Drive Step, coupled with the turning action of your hips and shoulders, creates the power behind the whip. This is a must-have strike in your personal defense arsenal. It's especially powerful for women, men, and teens alike, but it takes practice to perfect.

Knife-Hand Neck Strike

Strikes to the neck are only for the most serious threats and the Knife-Hand Neck Strike is no exception. It gets its name from the knife-like action caused by using the edge of your open palm to deliver the blow. A strike to the side of the neck, just below the earlobe on either side, crashes into the carotid artery, a major delivery highway for blood bringing oxygen to the larger, frontal part of your brain. This is the portion of the brain that affects your thinking, speech, and personality, as well as sensory and motor functions. You can feel your pulse in the carotid arteries on each side of your neck, right below the angle of the jawline.

The bullseye for this strike is the point where the carotid artery divides into the two lanes—the carotid sinus. A direct hit to the carotid sinus confuses the baroreceptors, sending a false distress signal to the brain that your blood pressure is rising rapidly. In response, your brain (connected to your heart through the Vagus nerve) directs the heart to slow down and lowers blood pressure. Fainting is common, and with a complete loss of body control, falling to the ground can result in serious head and neck injuries.

A proper Knife-Hand Neck Strike short circuits the carotid sinus
receptors, resulting in a loss of body control.

To execute an effective Knife-Hand Neck Strike, step to the right or left side of your assailant and use the arm on the same side as your step. Preferably your strike should be coming from your default "neutral stance," where your hands are up and in front of your chest. If you step with your right leg, thrust your elbow forward while turning the palm of your hand up toward the sky. Strike the side of the neck just in front and just below the earlobe. To make this strike the most effective, extend your hand (palm up) and rotate your hand at the wrist as far as it will comfortably go to the right. See how this creates a leading, hard edge to your strike? Use this two-inch edge of your palm heel (between the wrist and pinky finger) to strike the target. Turning your hand at the wrist as you deliver your strike naturally pulls the elbow the opposite direction, creating an instant whipping action. It also helps to protect your fingers from damage. You can also execute the Knife-Hand Neck Strike out of a left step and using the left arm. Turn your hand left at the wrist prior to the strike.

Knife-Hand Collarbone Strike

As I mentioned earlier, the clavicle (or collarbone) is particularly vulnerable to breaking; it's also extremely painful and debilitating to an opponent when it cracks. Snapping your assailant's collarbone is easy because: it's weak, we generally know where it's located, and it's often plainly visible, giving you a roughly 4-inch target to work with. Using the same open "knife hand" described above, simply strike *down* onto the collarbone with the lower heel/wrist portion of your palm. Remember to rotate your wrist up (or to the right) and strike down into the target (for added strength and protection to your hand). Deliver the blow with a quick downward "pop" to the collarbone. You'll be surprised how little power it takes to snap the bone, but don't test this theory or do your practicing on another person, except at slow motion speed. You may seriously hurt your practice partner with even the lightest impact to his or her collarbone.

The knife hand snaps down sharply using the heel of your wrist to cause the collarbone to break.

Brachial Stun

A strike to either side of the neck shocks the brachial plexus, a group of nerves that come from the spinal cord in the neck and travel down the arms. These nerves control the muscles of the shoulder, elbow, wrist, and hand, as well as the sense of feeling in the arms. The Brachial Stun is extremely effective, causing an immediate shock to an assailant that last roughly five seconds, and your assailant will fall.

A shot to the brachial nerves is effectively delivered using a quick "pop" to the neck in the space between the carotid artery and the earlobe. These nerves are located slightly further back on the neck than the carotid artery (where you were aiming with the Knife-Hand Neck Strike), so strike lower and deeper than you might think. If your right hand is dominant, strike the enemy from your left, with your palm facing down and turned as far left as possible at the wrist; this creates a leading hard edge to strike with—the two-inch space between the bottom of your wrist and below the pinkie finger. Facing your attacker, step deep with your left leg to the left side of your attacker, as you face him. As you step, whip your right wrist/heel into the opponent's brachial nerve with a quick, forceful pop.

Again, aim deeper, behind and below the earlobe to improve your chances of hitting the optimal spot. Unlike the Knife-hand Neck Strike, this strike uses a slight downward motion into the target area, which comes somewhat naturally when your palm is facing down and you're stepping to the left of your attacker.

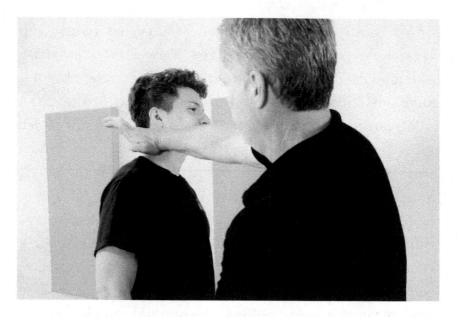

The Brachial Stun delivers a powerful blow with the heel of your wrist and palm. It's a deeper strike, between the carotid artery and the earlobe, disrupting muscle control.

You can strike the brachial nerve on the other side of the attacker as well; simply reverse the technique, using your right leg to step deep to the attacker's right side, and your left hand (palm facing down) to strike his brachial nerves.

Open-Palm Chin Strike

The Open-Palm Chin Strike can be delivered into the chin or under the jawline, using a variation of the open palm "knife hand" described above. The technique is simple, but it works best when you use the heel of your open palm to drive your strike into the target.

The Open-Palm Chin Strike allows for a devastating blow to the chin or jawline.

I prefer to keep my thumb slightly bent for added structure and strength. Imagine for a moment how an Olympic shot-putter holds onto the heavy, solid iron sphere as they launch it. It's almost like cradling a grapefruit with an open hand, but not so flat that it can roll out. The resulting curve in your palm creates a mini shovel, allowing for a devastating and painful blow if delivered up and into an opponent's chin or jawline with sufficient speed and power. This strike can be mastered quickly with some practice.

Nose Crush

This is another open-palm strike that is easy to learn and effective for temporarily disorienting your attacker. By driving the heel of your palm directly into his nose with sufficient force, the immediate effect is to stun your opponent, causing his eyes to tear up. After a minute or so, blood may start running down his nose, but by then, hopefully, you are long gone. Keep in mind, a strike to the nose is temporarily painful on impact, but most grown men will be able to shake it off and continue to attack. It's a great shot in a combination of strikes, but if it's your only strike, deliver it with enough force (as if you were pushing his nose several inches into his face) to enable a quick escape. Step directly in between the legs of your opponent using your same side leg and hand. If you're shorter than your target, the strike will naturally have an upward arc as your palm/heel plows into the assailant's nose.

The Nose Crush slams the heel of your palm several inches into the nose. Step and strike with the same side leg and arm; the elbow extends from the hip.

Hammer Hand

This strike is an exception to the open-palm strikes I usually prefer for shots to the neck and head. It's a closed-fist strike, but it's delivered using the side of your fist (which is naturally padded) instead of the front. If you can envision grasping a hammer and striking the butt of it across someone's jaw, you get the idea of the Hammer Hand. It's a powerful shot and has very minimal risk of injuring the bones in your wrist, hand, or fingers. Think about pounding on a door with the side of your fist in a hammering motion. It didn't hurt your hand, did it?

This technique uses a right-to-left or left-to-right motion depending on the arm you use. So, as you face your opponent, your right fist targets the left side of your opponent's jaw, sweeping from your left to right.

Clear a path for the Hammer Hand strike by first trapping the arm.

The Hammer Hand uses the side of your closed fist to strike at or near the jawline or ear.

Step to the outside of your opponent using your left leg to the left of the attacker while striking, elbow bent 90 degrees initially, and snapping open swiftly as you plant your foot into the ground. Use the side of your fist and wrist for whipping into the jawline between his ear and chin. The nice part is, even if you miss the jaw and hit too high toward the temple, or too low into the neck, the impact of your forearm is still likely to cause serious pain and disorientation. If you choose to attack using your left fist, step to the right side of your opponent with your right leg and whip your left fist into his jaw.

The Hammer Hand is amazingly powerful, even for people who aren't strong, because it uses the forward energy in your Drive Step to propel the whipping action of your opposite arm. And unlike the big, wide, haymaker hook that most people expect, the Hammer Hand comes in faster and tighter, making it much harder to block.

To clear a path for entry and add protection, trap or cover your opponent's hand on the side you are stepping towards as you strike the jawline using your free hand. It's not a grab of his hand; it's more like pushing it toward his body as you ring his bell up top! Finally, the Hammer Hand can be used as a horizontal strike (back fist) to the nose and is every bit as powerful as the Nose Crush.

EYE GOUGES AND JABS

Eye gouges and jabs are excruciatingly painful, can cause permanent damage to the eye of your attacker, and don't require any strength to execute effectively. The problem with an eye gouge is that it requires you to be in very close contact with the attacker, which probably means you're in serious trouble...so gouge as if your life depends upon it! Also, eye attacks aren't necessarily easy because the targets (the eyes) are very small and the head of your attacker is likely to be higher than yours and in motion (assuming there's a struggle). For these reasons, I teach new students a basic Double Thumb Eye Gouge and a Two Finger Eye Jab:

Double Thumbs

Double Thumb Eye Gouge

If both hands are free, this technique makes it virtually impossible to miss your attacker's eyes. Bring your palms together as if you were praying, then open your hands wide while keeping the wrists together. The width of the space between your open palms and fingers should roughly match the width of your attacker's head, while your two thumbs should be separated enough to slide over each side of his nose (the wrists stay together until just before the gouge). Thrust both elbows sharply forward, aiming your thumbs over the bridge of the nose and your hands past both ears. Continue the thrust as your thumbnails gouge deeply into his corneas.

Even if the attacker's head is moving, you can position your hands, being on both sides of his head, for direct thumb shots into the eyes! His hands will instantly come up to pull your wrists away. This is your opportunity to kick, knee, or roll him off and escape. Breaking his wrist grab is easy. Just flip your wrist sharply in the direction away from your body, the opposite motion when reading a wristwatch. If the attacker is too high for you to wrap your palms on either side of his head, use your fists to trap the chin from moving and your thumbs to gouge.

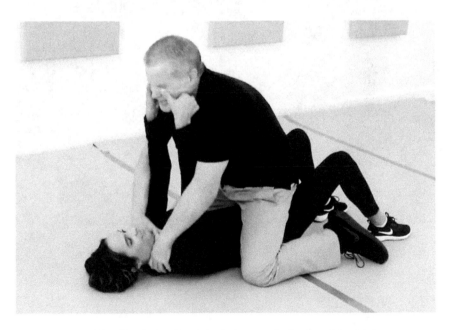

Double Thumb Eye Gouge technique used when reaching high.

Two Finger Eye Jab

Use your *first two* fingers to jab at the eye. Even if his head moves, and you only sweep the cornea with your fingernails, it's still incredibly painful.

Two Finger Eye Jab

CHOKEHOLDS

When it's your life or mine, chokes are a beautiful thing, unless you're the one being choked, of course (and in that case, nothing is more frightening and painful). These are two reasons why most people in a serious chokehold tend to give up the fight. Some chokes are designed to cut off the air supply to the lungs by clamping the windpipe (larynx), and this can lead to temporary unconsciousness within a minute, or—in rare cases—lead to death. This is why law enforcement officers are no longer permitted to use these types of chokeholds when arresting an uncooperative suspect. However, for the rest of us (in a life or death situation), any chokehold is fair.

Other types of chokes, though, can be used effectively to stop an attack or subdue a troublemaker without crushing his windpipe. These chokeholds are designed to cut off the blood supply to the brain by squeezing the carotid arteries running up either side of the neck. They work faster than chokes to the windpipe to render an attacker unconscious, usually in as little as 5-8 seconds. That's why one of the most common chokes is called a "sleeper," but it's closer to being a power nap in length, because the effects are temporary. So, don't stand over your vanquished opponent pounding your chest like a gorilla. Escape and call the police before he comes to life again. If the person goes unconscious and you release the pressure, you may have less than 30 seconds before he revives.

Several techniques that I use are hybrid chokes, such as the Full Double Carotid Choke, which cuts off both blood and oxygen supplies to the brain for a quicker end to any resistance. However, this chokehold (and others like it) is an advanced technique that requires some precision training to execute correctly and safely. For ease—and to prevent injury to your Kung Fu partner—I'll limit the chokeholds discussed in this book to the Rear Sleeper and the Lateral Choke. For experienced or very strong students, the choke techniques I've outlined may include a few more steps than necessary, but for beginners—or anyone up against a much taller or stronger assailant—the added steps are important to execute the chokeholds successfully.

But first, why use a chokehold at all? Why not just drive your fist into the belly or jaw and escape; it's faster and simpler? Well, first, chokeholds may be a better option than strikes in certain situations and a terrible choice in others, so, here's a summary.

Chokeholds are ideal if your objective is to:

- Overpower a much stronger aggressor or someone who has a higher tolerance for pain.

- Subdue and control your opponent to prevent or stop his harmful actions but without much risk to the aggressor of lasting pain or injury, or to cause bleeding or loss of other bodily fluids.

- Restrain the aggressor until help arrives. Keep him in the chokehold but back off of the full squeeze if he goes unconscious or if he complies with your instructions to stop resisting. Reapply the full squeeze if necessary.

- Surprise the aggressor by engaging from behind, or from his side when he's momentarily distracted. Or, in the case of the lateral chokehold, to use the element of surprise by rushing straight at the aggressor, which he will not expect.

Chokeholds are *not* suitable in the following situations:

- The aggressor is not alone (you'll be tied up with the first guy and vulnerable to attack from his buddy).

- If a weapon is showing. Even if you're behind the aggressor, you can easily be shot or stabbed before he loses consciousness. There are advanced variations on the chokehold for this circumstance, but they are not discussed in this book.

- The aggressor is substantially taller (more than a six-inch difference in height may make it difficult to secure a chokehold and throw off his balance).

Rear Sleeper Chokehold

If you can't immediately engage your attacker from behind, you'll need an "entry" move to position yourself for a rear chokehold. One approach to gain position is to take a big left Drive Step, deep enough to align your left foot with your opponent's foot on the same side. Your head (and weight) should be directly over your left foot. Place one hand on each of your opponent's shoulders as you step to his left (this provides you with balance and helps to keep your opponent from spinning out of the entry move).

Next, drag your trailing (right) leg up to your other foot and then use it to make one or two small "shuffle" steps to pivot yourself in position behind your opponent. Now, wedge the crook of your right forearm under his chin while stepping between your opponent's legs and driving your right hip into his tailbone. Simultaneously, use your left hand to push into the small of his back (this effectively takes away your opponent's balance and, if he's taller, lowers his shoulders to make for an easier choke to the neck. After the quick push to lower back, bring your left arm up and wrap it *behind* your opponent's neck. Once you have a secure chokehold in place, immediately squat down, taking a small step or two back and pulling your opponent down in a controlled manner—essentially resting his tailbone on your nearest thigh.

Now, while maintaining your chokehold, drop your free leg down to one knee and let your opponent's tailbone slide off your thigh and onto the ground. Lean your weight into your opponent while you squeeze his neck using your core muscles for the choke (like a sit up, and this will give you much more strength than using your biceps alone).

You now have complete control of your opponent. Apply sufficient pressure around the neck to gain cooperation, but no more. With practice, the entire technique—from entry to a controlled chokehold while lowering to one knee—should take no longer than five seconds. The chokehold steps described throughout this section assume a dominant right hand but any of the chokes can be initiated from either side.

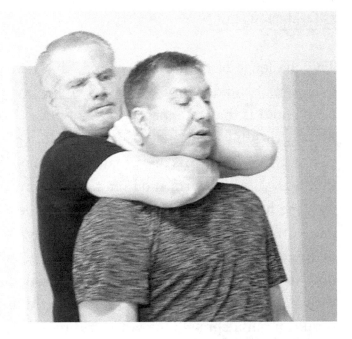

Proper arm placement for a Rear Sleeper Chokehold.

Of course, it's quicker and easier if you can engage your attacker from directly behind him, and it brings the element of surprise. In this scenario, step your right leg forcefully between the legs of your opponent and drive your right hip into his tailbone. Simultaneously, whip your right arm around his neck until the crook of your forearm is wedged under his chin. Use your left hand to push into the small of his back to take him off balance, and then lower your weight by squatting. Bring your left arm up and wrap it *behind* your opponent's neck. Finally, lean into your opponent while squeezing your core muscles to apply sufficient force to the choke to gain compliance.

Lateral Chokehold

The challenge of the Rear Sleeper is that it requires you to maneuver behind your opponent. The beauty of the Lateral Chokehold is that you attack your opponent from the front. Start with a big right step to his left side while using your right arm to slam across his throat, essentially "clotheslining" him with your right arm and then taking away his balance by pushing his right elbow forward with your left hand as you maneuver past his left side. Continuing your forward momentum, "walk" your opponent to the ground by taking four steps past him, lowering yourself closer to the ground with each step and landing on your right hip. Your legs should be in a sprawl (like you're riding a bicycle, with the right leg in front of the left), preventing your opponent from turning his body and escaping or reversing your chokehold. Now, apply your left arm across the back of his neck to secure a double-arm choke. Once both arms and legs are in position, squeeze the neck using your lower bicep tendons to provide a firm grip, but use your abdominal core for the application of the choke—squeezing your core like a tight sit up.

Step 1: Step to the left of your assailant with your right leg while slamming your right forearm into his throat.

Step 2: As your left leg continues forward, lower your weight while pushing your left hand forward into his elbow.

Step 3: Walk the assailant to the ground in a controlled manner and position your legs into a sprawl (like riding a bike with your right leg forward and left leg back) to prevent escape.

Step 4: Clinch the chokehold with your left hand over your right wrist. Apply the choke by squeezing your core (like a sit up), which is more powerful than your biceps alone. Turn your head away to prevent the assailant from reaching your face with his hands.

As you apply the necessary force from your abdomen to subdue the assailant, jam his head into the ground with the top of your forearm and shoulder. He'll be in a lot of pain at this point, with virtually no chance of escape. Be sure to turn your head away from the assailant during the application of the squeeze to prevent him from reaching your face with his hands before he's subdued.

ESCAPING A REAR CHOKE

There are several fairly easy ways to escape a choke from the rear, but in all of them, the faster you react when you're first grabbed, the better your chances of a quick escape. In all situations, tucking your chin immediately helps to prevent the strongest chokehold to be applied, but far more important is reacting the split-second you feel an arm coming around your shoulder and neck. Hesitation gives the attacker time to push you off balance, putting you in a far more difficult situation. The following are three of my recommended escapes:

Thrusting Elbow

This escape begins by turning *into* your opponent while repeatedly striking your elbow into his gut using the same-side elbow as the direction of your turn. During the turn, aim a little higher with each rapid-fire elbow thrust (creating space between you) and finish him off with an elbow to the jaw.

Thrusting Elbow rear choke escape.

Shoulder Turn

Tuck your chin and quickly turn yourself 180-degrees into your attacker, leading with either shoulder. Drop your weight slightly as you turn to slip the grip. Create space between you with an elbow to the chest and drive your fist into his body.

Shoulder Turn Escape. Sequence shown from left to right, top to bottom.

Single Knee Drop

The Single Knee Drop is easy to execute. Use a double grab to your attacker's choke arm and drop one knee to the ground. At the same time, drop your shoulder on the same side as your dropping knee and your attacker will flip over you. Staying attached throughout the flip, you'll end up with your opponent's right arm trapped under your left arm pit. This takes away his use of the arm as a weapon, and you can pummel him with open strikes to the jaw and nose, or a backhanded fist to the ear and jawline. Alternatively, release the trapped arm after the flip and escape immediately. One downside to the Single Knee Drop is the potential for shattering your kneecap if you slam it down into the ground. While practicing the knee drop, use your toes to slow the force onto your knee just prior to impact.

Single Knee Drop escape from a rear choke.

ESSENTIAL BLOCKS & COUNTER ATTACKS

You now know that attacking first whenever possible is a major advantage against a threat. The moment of attack, the reach of your strikes or kicks, and your speed and power are all unknown to the attacker. You now also know how to be more aware of your environment and the individuals around you, and you know how to ready yourself if a threatening person crosses your path. Critically, you know what to do if the tension can't be deescalated and the threat steps into your attack zone. Nevertheless, mistakes happen and bad people get lucky too. You can find yourself blindsided by a punch to the head, tackled to the sidewalk, or taking on a furious cycle of punches from someone whom you didn't detect as a possible threat. Now, the bad guy took advantage of the first attack and you're on the defensive.

Our defensive and countering techniques are designed for just this type of scenario. You screwed up—you did! Letting someone else strike or tackle you first is a mistake, but it isn't the end of the fight. I'll share with you now some of my most effective defensive techniques. They're not difficult to learn but they do require some practice, and the more you practice and perfect these techniques, the more reliable and effective they'll be when you need them most.

As I stated before, when it comes to training, it's always helpful to have a Kung Fu partner, especially on defensive moves—someone who will bring in some resistance, realism, and the unexpected. Again, start each technique very slowly, walking through each move, first in the air, and then eventually with your Kung Fu partner.

Head Movement

I hate spiders, and I always make a joke to my students that the fastest I've ever moved my head was whenever I've found myself suddenly tangled with a cobweb on my face or in my hair. The point is that your head can move as fast as you want it to. If you ever look at the most successful boxers both past and present, like Canelo Alvarez, their head movement is so smooth and effective that they can fight an entire round without using their arms to block a punch, only relying on their head movement to evade incoming strikes.

It seems like common sense to move your head back and away from danger; your brain automatically responds to incoming objects in this way. But in a street fight, the better defense is to move your head down. This is a skill that requires some coaching and practice. For all of us who don't have the natural head movement of Canelo Alvarez, the best way to block, counter, or evade incoming strikes is to raise your arm to deflect the blow, lowering your head in that split second, and bringing your balance and energy forward, not backward. It may seem like a lot of things to do, but once you've learned some simple arm blocks, lowering your head and leaning forward will become more natural and automatic.

A boxer prepares to fight by fighting (sparring), but the martial artist performs drills that are rehearsed and, surprisingly, don't include simple head movements for defense. In contrast, I've taken basic head movements used in boxing and integrated them into my self-protection system, and it works beautifully. This will not only protect your pretty face, but moving your head down a few inches—ultimately lowering your center of gravity—also protects from incoming strikes to the body. When people attack, rarely is it with one powerful shot; it's usually a flurry of fists. By lowering your head, you simultaneously protect both the head and the body by making yourself a "smaller" target and leaving fewer and tighter areas for an incoming blow to land effectively.

Having that lowered forward energy is also essential for creating the balance and leverage needed to throw devastating counter strikes and attack the person coming at you. Just by lifting your hand to the crown of your head to block the blow creates lowered forward energy. With practice, your coordinated blocks with head movements will speed up, become more forward, and will naturally flow into counter punching.

Wedge Block

The most common punch thrown on the face of the earth is called a "haymaker," an exaggerated, goofy looking right hook to the head. Just about everyone who has been in a fight but never had any training throws these monstrous hooks, and they do it by telegraphing their intentions in a way that is completely obvious to anyone with an even a small amount of training. Most people believe that a huge windup is necessary in a punch if you want to deliver power. And since nine out ten people you'll ever face in a fight are right-handed, 90% of all punches will be thrown at you from your left. Now that you have a pretty good idea of where a potential punch might be coming from initially, it's easier to watch for the telltale signs of the start of the punch with the inevitable windup. Many amateurs look away momentarily —as if they're trying to keep their composure, and thinking of a way to settle the matter. Instead, they're counting on a split-second opening where you'll be thinking that the situation is de-escalating and let your guard down. And then here comes the haymaker! His right shoulder dips down and backward as he initiates the windup, and his head dips slightly in unison with the shoulders. His elbow travels backward, then forward, as his right shoulder rises and the punch comes circling around like one of Saturn's rings.

Single-Arm Wedge Block with simultaneous Solar Plexus Strike

It may look like the punch was thrown in a split-second on a YouTube street fight video, and it probably was, but to anyone with a bit of training, it's slow, predictable, and easy to block. One very effective block against the Haymaker is what I call the "Wedge Block." The Wedge Block is an extension of a basic Wing Chun block called "Bil Sao," where your arm (on the same side as the incoming punch) is extended to about three-quarters distance from your body, firing rapidly into the oncoming strike and intercepting it with your forearm at or just above his elbow. It's an amazingly effective block that can stop even the strongest of punches headed for your face. The secret is in the added structure and force created from the alignment of the shoulder, elbow, wrist, and hand, as well as the force from stepping into the attacking arm with your same-side leg.

Effective alignment requires that the hand should be pointed away from your body at the wrist, whether blocking with your left or right arm. This also has the effect of pushing your elbow in the opposite direction; and the benefit is that you now have a remarkably solid structure (your arm and shoulder) that is nearly impossible to pass through! Your target for the block is much larger too. Blocking the attacking arm gives you a wide surface to intercept before it becomes a very small target—a fist to your face. While stepping directly toward your attacker, lower your weight for stability and your head for protection. By intercepting the incoming punch with your wedge block, the haymaker punch becomes a dud instead. With his primary weapon launched and blocked, you're positioned directly in front of his exposed body with an available right fist. Use it. In Kuaishou instruction, my students learn to be very efficient fighters: with every block comes a simultaneous strike, followed by several more strikes. It takes practice to block and strike simultaneously, but when proficient it's wickedly effective at ending fights instantly, and your adversary will literally never know what hit them.

Double-Arm Wedge Block

Smaller and lighter people facing a much larger and stronger attacker should use the easier Double-Arm Wedge Block until they've had sufficient training to use the Single-Arm Wedge block.

Double-Arm Wedge Block

Simply step into the direction of the incoming punch and thrust both forearms arms into the opponent's incoming arm, preferably one below and one above his elbow. Lower your head and use your forearms, your big step, and the forward energy it brings, to block the punch. After the punch fails, and with your hands still raised, whip a Hammer Hand to his ear with the side of a closed fist, using the hand closest to his head. It's a straight line, and it'll be unprotected and unexpected!

Ear Cover

Of course, not every punch comes in as wide and as predictable as the Haymaker, or maybe you reacted a split second too late to block the Haymaker with a Wedge block. Not to worry. That same hand you should've used to intercept the strike can be pulled up even quicker next to your ear, using your hand, forearm, elbow, and bicep to blunt the force of the incoming punch.

Single-Arm Ear Cover Block with simultaneous strike to the solar plexus

Almost any amount of cover helps soften the blow, but

the ideal protection is tight and up against your head; your arm essentially looks like you're flexing your bicep, with your hand covering the ear. As you pull your arm into position, drop your weight straight down (but don't bend at the waist) and tuck your head by bringing your chin into your armpit on the same side as the Ear Cover Block. Keep your eyes looking forward enough to spot open targets for counter strikes and to also to keep an eye on your opponent's left hand.

With some practice, you should easily be able to deliver a counter strike into your opponent before his left punch launches, impacting his balance, diminishing his power, and throwing off his aim.

Double-Ear Cover and Countering

This is the same block described above but covering both sides of the head at the same time. We call this the "Oh Sh#t block" because it means you're taking a firestorm of punches and you're forced to go completely defensive in protecting yourself. With both arms covering either side of your head, drop your weight straight down to help protect your body and maintain balance. There are several good counter-moves you can use to turn the tables on the incoming hellfire. One of my favorites is the Attacking Forearm, previously demonstrated. You've already lowered your weight; now take a deep attack step right between your opponent's legs and drive your forearm across his chest to launch your counter attack. His punches will either be deflected by your incoming forearm or miss past your head, and you'll be throwing him off balance as well. Immediately attack with your own strikes.

Double-Ear Cover Block

Countering a surprise flury of punches. Step 1: Protect your head with a Double-Ear Cover Block.

Step 2: Lower your body to get underneath the blows, and then lunge.

Step 3: After the Forearm Strike, you can escape or immediately go into attack mode with a combination of strikes.

KICKS

Kicks are a valuable tool to have in your self-protection arsenal, particularly for women, who tend to have greater lower body strength compared to the upper body. But kicks can be tricky to use in a street fight unless you've had some training. Under an avalanche of adrenaline (as you will be in a serious altercation), it's far more difficult to maintain your balance during a kick than it is in the relative calm and controlled conditions of the gym. Moreover, the ground may be uneven or even wet and slippery, and kicks from people with no training are susceptible to being caught with the opponent's hand. This invariably means you'll be flat on your back on the ground in a couple of seconds, potentially landing with your head and neck first.

With these cautions in mind, there are a couple of kicks that everyone should learn and practice. The Front Kick is common to many martial art systems, but you'll maintain better balance and power if you keep your kicks low—no higher than the attacker's belly. High Kicks in a street fight are ridiculous, especially spinning kicks to the head. (Since these require expert balance, precision targeting, and taking your eyes off your opponent to execute, save them for a Hollywood movie or your Kickboxing competition, not a street fight.) The Front Kick is also effective when you're flat on your back or up against a wall and trying to force an attacker off of you. The surface behind your back and hips adds even more power to the kick. I also like the Knee Destruction Kick, which is devastating. It's very difficult for your opponent to see it coming and leaves the attacker with serious knee-joint damage. Your escape after landing this kick won't allow for a chase.

Front Kick

The Front Kick can be executed with either your lead leg or your reverse (rear leg), although most beginners will find it easier when using the reverse leg. The absolute key to an effective front kick (or any kick) is properly chambering your kicking leg before releasing the kick. To properly chamber the leg, raise your knee straight up until it is at least parallel to the ground, if not more. After chambering, extend your kicking leg toward the belly, striking with the entire flat of your foot. As with punches, kick with enough force to send your heel several inches into the belly before retracting. Kicking higher into the chest requires more skilled balance and can make the kick easier to intercept. Kicking lower into the groin is effective, but easier to miss, often landing on or partially onto the thigh instead and lessening the pain. The belly, on the other hand, is an easy target to hit, low enough to maintain adequate balance, and very effective for knocking the wind out of an attacker.

The Front Kick works best when you chamber the knee high before moving the leg forward, kicking flat-footed.

Knee Destruction Kick

This kick takes more practice, but it's worth it. The name pretty much describes the purpose of this kick, so use it only where the injury you'll deliver is consistent with the threat. Like all kicks I teach, chambering the knee properly (as discussed above) is essential for maximum power and precise delivery. With both hands up and in the "ready" position, chamber your leg high and kick down, aiming for the top of the kneecap. As your kick descends, turn your ankle to the outside (to the left on your left leg or to the right on your right leg).

Knee Destruction Kicks are devastating if you chamber the knee high before kicking and drive down onto the top of the kneecap.

The degree of the turn should be roughly 11:00 on the clock dial for your left foot and 1:00 for your right. Again, don't get in the habit of turning your ankle as you lift your leg to chamber. Instead, turn the foot once you've started the kick downward. Turning the foot too soon will result in your hips opening way too wide (you'll be exposed, off-balance, and your kick will miss). On the downward motion of your chambering leg, aim just above the kneecap of your attacker and drive the heel of your foot down into the target. Kick through the target several inches. The resulting strike will not only be very painful, it will cause severe damage to the ligaments and the cartilage supporting the knee, and your attacker will be unable and unwilling to pursue you any further. If he had a tennis career, that's over too!

With kicks, I often get asked which leg should be used to kick, which leg on the opponent should be targeted, and if either even makes a difference. First, let's talk about which leg to use to strike. Most people feel more comfortable kicking with their dominant leg, but not all. I know plenty of right-handers that impressively kick the heavy bag with their left leg and are noticeably weaker when using their right leg. Try it out for yourself and see what feels more natural and powerful for you. As with any technique, mastering its use from either side is the goal, but if you know ahead of time what works best (and you have the option to choose), going to your strong side is obviously advantageous.

With respect to the target, a good rule of thumb is to attack whatever knee is closest to you, but with kicks you also need to consider the circumstances. Kicks require a certain amount of distance between the kicker and the target. The clearance needed for your knee to be parallel to the ground when chambering is obviously the minimum amount of space necessary, but if your attacker's mirror image leg is in a lead position, it could be too close for the force of your kick to do major damage. Steer your kick to the trailing (furthest) leg instead and give yourself some runway to deliver a powerful, downward blow to the knee. If his trailing leg is out of reach, then chances are, your opponent's balance is already compromised. Take a step back if necessary to create some space, feint (fake) a strike to the head to distract him, and then attack his lead leg.

KNEES

Knees are effective weapons, but typically require you to be physically attached to your attacker to maintain balance and generate maximum power. In effect, you're already at a disadvantage with the attack happening and with no distance between you. One of my knee techniques, the Attacking Knee, eliminates the need to be physically attached to your opponent, and I recommend it to everyone, but particularly to women, who can also use it to exploit their lower body strength.

Attacking Knee

The Attacking Knee uses the same leg chambering technique as the kicks described above, as well as the same forward energy found in the Attacking Forearm. If using your dominant leg for the knee strike, step deeply and directly toward your opponent, roughly 12-18" in front of your target. While making your attack step, your trailing leg follows until it chambers to the point where your thigh is parallel to the floor. Instead of kicking, drive the front of your knee six inches into your opponent's belly, groin, lower ribs, or liver using the momentum from your initial attack step to power your hips and knee forward. It's like a having a third fist to hit with and there's no need to grab onto the person. This knee is especially useful if you need to defend yourself from someone you'd rather not touch or risk transferring body fluids with, such as an aggressive, unkempt homeless person, or someone appearing to be strung out on drugs.

The Attacking Knee requires no grabbing of your opponent for power.

COMBINATION STRIKES

Any one of the singular strikes discussed above can end a fight instantly, but I always teach my students to strike in combinations, for several reasons. Insurance is the primary purpose of a second (or third, or fourth) shot. Maybe the first punch didn't land exactly where intended, or with sufficient power? You want to be ready to immediately launch another shot or two just in case.

Another reason for throwing combinations is your body's natural balance. Keeping both hands up and using continuously fluid motions helps maintain your balance and improve speed, and it gives you the ability to block an incoming punch if required. Lastly, there's a certain rhythm to boxing, just as there is in dancing, where you have two feet that need to move in a coordinated fashion. It's the same with your hands (and feet) in fighting. By firing off two strikes, one after the other, your natural rhythm and balance is maintained. It's on the third strike during combinations that I see the most fall-off in power from my students. This has mostly to do with footwork and proper body movement. It's OK—the more you practice your combinations (preferably with some experienced instruction), the faster, harder, and more even-powered your strikes will become, be it a combination of two or twelve strikes.

Since we've already introduced you to six standalone strikes, adding a second punch isn't going to take much more basic instruction. Any combination of jabs, hooks, or head and neck shots can be effective if you exploit what your opponent gives you. By practicing combinations that go both low and high, you'll train yourself to take advantage of an attacker shielding his head (leaving the body exposed) or conversely, protecting his body (leaving the head and neck exposed). Except for those with some training, most people automatically respond to a shot to the face by covering their head with both hands, and the same is true for the guy who brings both hands to his belly after being whacked in the gut. Unless you're expecting the punch (and bracing for it), it's a hard habit to break without practice.

In Kuaishou, my own system, there are 16 different and numbered strikes using a fist or open hand. Therefore, the various combinations of these strikes are in the hundreds. For simplicity, I'll limit each combination here in the book at two strikes.

Solar Plexus + Palm Strike

For this combination, step deep and straight between your opponent's legs while delivering a vertical fist into his solar plexus, then follow it up with an open-hand strike with your free hand to his jawline. If his head bucks forward from the body shot and you end up striking past his jaw, that's OK too. They both were unexpected and they both hurt.

Liver + Ribs

This combination stays at the body, targeting two vulnerable and painful body parts: the floating ribs and the liver. I like the Drive Step to your attacker's left, targeting the liver with your right horizontal fist, followed by a quick left into his lower ribs. Picture Rocky Balboa in the cooler attacking the hanging meat. This body combination also naturally keeps you low to your opponent, making it that much more difficult for him to find a worthy target on you!

Ear Whip + Belly

You can do this combination from either side, but I do like the extra power that comes from the automatic hip turn when you attack with an Ear Whip out of the Drive Step. As you step to his left, your right (open-handed) palm heel whips into your attacker's ear. He'll now be staggering before your second shot goes off, so just aim for the belly instead of trying to be too precise. You can't miss! Drive that left horizontal hook into his gut. If you hit his lower ribs or liver, so much the better!

MULTIPLE ATTACKERS

Finally, remember the story of Monica, the 5'2" young woman who had been encircled by a group of football players from her high school team and assaulted by them? She could have used any of these techniques successfully. But against whom? After all, there were many potential assailants. While this is true, the same dynamics are at play in virtually every multiple-attacker situation: one guy is the ring leader, one or two more guys are his tough talking associates, and the rest of them are there to act cool, but won't fight. In a multiple threat situation, deliver a speedy dose of pure pain to the attacker who is closest to you and let his friends watch him crumple to the ground. If it's the leader, that's even better. Chances are the others will retreat because it's not really their fight in the first place. If you recall in Monica's situation, the ringleader was Chad, the quarterback of the team. Had Monica inflicted excruciating pain on any of them, but particularly on Chad, none of the other idiots were then going to challenge Monica. With nothing to gain, the pain, shock, and humiliation would have quickly driven them all away.

There are exceptions to every rule, of course, and that's why we like watching Jack Reacher take on a handful of street thugs, decimating most of them and watching the last guy standing run away. Multiple attackers, especially in street gang conflicts, may be forced to jump in and help their buddy or face dire consequences from the gang leaders for their lack of loyalty and courage. For this reason, here are a few tips when facing multiple threats:

- Get your back up against a wall, fence, car, or counter if it enables you to keep all attackers in your field of vision.

- Don't use techniques that will tie you up with one assailant, such as chokeholds, stand-up grappling, or any ground fighting (Jiu-Jitsu).

- Take out the person closest to you before any attack begins. Use surprise, speed, and overwhelming fury to your advantage. The first guy should be out of the game with a quick two-punch combination. Immediately attack the next closest threat.

- Pick up the spare. As in bowling, knocking down multiple pins with a single toss is key. Same with fighting multiple attackers. An Attacking Forearm to the chest area will blow back an assailant ten-feet or more. Drive him into one or more in the group and then kick them in the side of the head or ribs if they try to get up.

- Always assume the other person(s) may have a knife or gun on them. Watch their hands if they reach into their coat, waist, or under their pant cuff. Attack the weapon first, not the person.

- Breathe. Keeping a controlled, steady flow of oxygen into your lungs will allow you to perform at your peak. Too many people forget to breath when they're under attack, or they do the exact opposite and hyperventilate. Neither of them works for long.

8

WEAPONS

As trusting as I am of my techniques and training, there's a practical use for weapons in self-protection, though none of them are a singular substitute for proper self-defense training. Let's start with the obvious—to use a weapon, you have to have it on or near you when needed. Think about your daily routine, all the places you go, and the vehicles you use to get there. Having an effective weapon handy all the time isn't practical, especially if you live in a state with no "open carry" law. Students aren't permitted to bring weapons to school. Passengers can't bring weapons on an airplane. Fans can't bring weapons into a stadium or concert. And retrieving a weapon in a split-second is more difficult than you might think. The exceptions to all of these are your hands and feet, which are always with you, and can be deployed quickly and powerfully in a fraction of a second. They are always your best, everyday weapons.

Owning virtually any weapon carries a risk that it could bring harm to someone or yourself unintentionally. That said, some weapons are far safer to own and use than others. At the end of the day, owning a weapon for self-defense is a personal choice, and this chapter is designed as an overview of options to consider, including firearms, knives, batons, and sprays, as well as improvised weapons, both contrived and found in the moment of attack.

FIREARMS

Two-thirds of Americans choose not to own a gun, can't afford one, or haven't thought about it. I happen to own a gun, but it's not my first choice for self-protection purposes, and there's no way that I'd keep it in a bedroom drawer where it could easily be found or stolen. Instead, I keep it locked in a safe, not just to keep a burglar from taking it, but because, sadly, 4.6 million of our children under 18 years old live in a home with at least one gun that is loaded and unlocked! And while parents may think they've done an adequate job of hiding their gun, one study revealed that 22% of kids surveyed separately from their parents knew where the gun was located and have handled the weapon unsupervised. As a result, 1,300 children are killed by accidental gunshots every year, and in 82% of youth suicides where a gun was used, the weapon of choice was found in their own home.[18]

While about half of gun owners report having a firearm for self-defense purposes, the latest data show that people use guns for self-defense only rarely. According to a Harvard University analysis of figures from the National Crime Victimization Survey, people defended themselves with a gun in less than 0.9 percent of crimes during the five-year period from 2007 to 2011. While your chances of ever needing a gun to defend yourself in your lifetime are exceedingly small, the opportunity exists every day that a gun in your home can be mishandled, used on an innocent victim, or stolen. Recently, a Los Angeles man—a veteran—shot and killed an intruder in his home who was attacking his 11-year-old son. How can you argue that owning a gun in this instance wasn't a blessing? Unfortunately, when the police arrived, they fatally shot the boy's father when he failed to heed their commands to drop his own weapon. Turns out, the father had severe hearing issues from his time in military service, and it cost him his life—an absolute tragedy.

Nevertheless, many people feel more secure owning a firearm, and if everyone who owned guns was responsible, properly trained, secured the weapon safely, and was mentally stable, nobody would even argue with their decision or their constitutional right. If purchasing a firearm is your choice, my personal preference for self-protection is either a .38 caliber or .357-magnum handgun or a shotgun. The .38 Special is very popular, particularly among those who prefer simplicity in a revolver. It is easy to use, inexpensive, and available in a wide variety of configurations. Another popular choice is the .357 Magnum, a weapon where its reputation for stopping bad people from doing bad things is well-deserved. It's a larger gun, but for home defense, heavier, larger guns absorb recoil more easily, and its longer sight radius makes it easier to be precise in hitting your intended target. Both the .38 and .357 are revolvers, which rarely jam, as opposed to the 9mm, .40 caliber, or .45 caliber semi-automatic pistols, which must be chambered. These pistols use a closed bolt system with ammunition clips that are susceptible to jamming.

Semi-automatic pistols hold 15-18 bullets in a magazine, making them of dire necessity for law enforcement engaged in a firefight. For home protection, however, you'll need only a few pulls of the trigger from a revolver to end the threat, and with five or six bullets in your revolver, it stills leaves you with a few to spare.

Shotguns are ideal for close quarters contact, making them a popular choice for a home defense weapon. The standard 00 buckshot shell sprays nine .33 caliber projectiles at your intruder at velocities well above those of most handguns, greatly increasing the chances of hitting vital organs and stopping a threat immediately. Pump action and semi-automatic action shotguns are the only two that are practical for home defense, because they are the fastest forms of operation for a shotgun. The 12-gauge shotgun is more powerful, but it's also larger, heavier, and recoils fiercely. A 20-gauge shotgun is still a very potent round and is much friendlier for smaller people.

If a firearm is something you're considering for self-protection, visit a licensed, reputable gun dealer and have a knowledgeable sales professional walk you through the best options for you. Be sure to get professional safety and target training, and properly secure the weapon when not in use.

BATONS

If you want an easier, safer, and less expensive weapon for self-protection, I would recommend either a hardwood or heavy-duty expandable baton. All things considered, a baton is in my opinion the best overall weapon for self-protection at home. A reasonably priced 22"-26" maple or ash baton costs between $30 - $60. For a hardwood baton, there is no reason to get one larger than 26"; its weight will become an issue when swinging it, especially for a smaller person. Batons made from tropical South American hardwood are made with the world's hardest woods and many of them are beautiful to look at, but pricier, up to $100 or more.

There are also expandable (telescopic) steel and carbon batons. A 12" carbon baton fully expands to 21" or 22" inches within a split second upon the press of a lever and a flick of your wrist. High-quality models usually sell for $75 to $125 or more. I've tested less expensive options and they're suscep-tible to falling apart and can easily bend on impact. While batons are completely legal to have in your home, they're illegal to carry with you or to transport (other than in the locked trunk of your car) in most states. There are permits available to carry a baton in certain circumstances, such as security and law enforcement purposes, and some states with Concealed Handgun Permits allow batons with the same permit. In general, the more rural states tend to allow you to carry a baton, while the more populated states make it illegal outside of the home.

I love batons because they are easy to use; it will take less than a couple of hours of practice for you to be effective and comfortable with it. And when it's used properly, you'll be able to sufficiently incapacitate your assailant without killing them. Also, the chance of an accidental tragedy is lessened significantly. You can keep it safely next to your bed or by the front door.

Holding the baton correctly, you'll have about 16" of usable, exposed wood or carbon with which to strike, and this is more than sufficient. With this baton length, you can cause massive pain and cripple your assailant by striking his kneecap—causing the kneecap to shatter—or smashing his upper Tibia/Fibula and breaking his leg with the blunt force. Similarly, a double-arm thrust to the abdomen, liver, and kidneys is extremely effective. Regardless, you'll only need to minimally retract the baton whether you're using it for a thrust or strike because of the weight and force of the baton. Depending on the area of the body you're striking, only small movements of the baton are necessary to cause brutal, intense pain that will drop and render any assailant harmless.

Additionally, you don't need to be extremely accurate in your strike or thrust. If you aren't precise, you will still inflict severe pain and put your assailant on the ground, even if you don't break anything. You can also use the nub or heel of the baton, which is usually about 4-6". This end of the baton is easier to thrust into the gut and to jam into the ribs and kidneys as a second strike after an initial attack strike.

Finally, with one exception, I do not recommend baseball bats for self-protection. Like a baton, bats are considered deadly weapons, and in many states, can only be legally transported in the trunk of your car (a law enforcement friend of mine suggests always having a baseball glove with your baseball bat in a car to avoid the potential of a fine or arrest for carrying a deadly weapon without a permit). For home protection, most bats are too long and too heavy. As a result, you're likely to strike walls, doorjambs, windows, and furniture when you swing a full-sized bat in your house. Also, bats are relatively easy to block and disarm from the user. If you don't believe me, watch my online video on baseball bats, part of my series on *Baton Basics* by Defense Kinetics on YouTube. The shorter baton can deliver 2-3 times the amount of strikes in the same time it takes for a single swing of a bat. The exception to recreational bats being a less effective home defense weapon is the 26" aluminum youth T-Ball bat. There are 13 oz. versions that sell for $10 to $25. These ultra-lightweight bats are made with military-grade rolled aluminum, are incredibly strong, and can deliver serious blows to an intruder. Choke up about one hand length up the grip and use it just as you would a hardwood or carbon baton. The heel end of the kid's bat is not as effective as a baton for thrusting shots into the body (due to the rounded knob end), but for strikes to the lower legs, hands, and arms, this harmless looking T-ball bat can easily break bones.

EDGED WEAPONS

Knives and other edged weapons are designed to be lethal; their purpose is to puncture arteries and vital organs—and this is why they are so effective for self-protection. After all, you're not using it to threaten an assailant with a severe cut on his forearm. A serious stabbing wound to the gut (intestinal perforation) can cause intense bleeding and massive infection. The resulting sepsis can be overwhelming and often fatal, even with the most aggressive treatment. Puncture wounds to the carotid arteries in the neck and femur bleed out quickly and are often fatal without immediate medical attention.

Nevertheless, a knife is a safer weapon to own than a gun because the chance of accidental death is far less. One challenge with a knife is that you need to be extremely close to your assailant to use it (by comparison, you'll have an extra two feet of space between you and an assailant with a baton). Of course, this assumes that you aren't planning on tossing the knife at your assailant, which, by the way, is a terrible idea, unless you're an expert, or perhaps desperate. That all said, in my training, I do teach the effective use of knives as an attacking weapon, as well as how to defend against a knife attack. I teach only thrust puncture strikes, not the slashing techniques favored by most fighting arts. It's not about looking cool with slashing figure 8's in the air. Knives are for thrusting violently into an assailant, preferably into the gut (which is below the assailant's vision line). Their sole purpose is to deliver a lethal attack on someone intent on doing you serious harm.

Knife defense techniques are effective but they take more advanced training to be reliable in a real-life encounter, where the weapon could end up in your intestines before you ever saw it coming. It's another reason why I teach my students to always assume an attacker has a weapon, even if you see that both hands are empty. If you spot an attacker's empty hand disappear for even a fraction of a second, attack the wrist of their returning hand before it starts to move toward your body.

Being proficient in both offensive and defensive edged weapons takes about 20 hours of training. But once you know how to use one effectively, keeping a nice $40 collapsible knife with a 4" blade in your car is a viable and legal option. You can even carry it on your person so long as it's not exposed. Similarly, a six-inch, twenty-dollar, military-style fixed blade (K-Bar) knife is a good option for your home, but illegal to have in your car.

PEPPER SPRAYS

My biggest concern about pepper spray or mace (a brand of pepper spray with the same active ingredients) is that far too many people rely on it as their *sole means* for self-protection. Effectively subduing an assailant with spray is more difficult than you think. Under ideal conditions, it takes about 1.5 seconds to retrieve pepper spray from a pocket or purse, which means you'll need to identify the potential assailant at about 20 feet away and deploy the spray within 10 feet to hit your target. You may, or may not, have the luxury of that amount of time, and it's never going to be ideal conditions. There's also the possibility that if deployed in an enclosed space, like a car or elevator, you'll come in contact with the irritant as well.

Instead, I prefer using sprays proactively rather than

reactively, and as a deterrent. Should you find yourself in a dimly lit parking garage, for example, or waiting at the side of the road for a tow truck to arrive, having the spray in your hand and ready to deploy is a smart and practical option. It's also handy if confronted by an aggressive panhandler or other individual, where just showing the spray should be enough to get them to back off. It is legal in all 50 states to carry and use pepper spray for self-defense purposes, although certain jurisdictions restrict the size of the container.

Lastly, pepper spray is an effective deterrent to a dog attack. However, sprays designed specifically for dog attacks aren't recommended for use on humans because they tend to be less potent. In summary, use pepper spray or mace as just one weapon in your self-protection toolbox.

CONTRIVED IMPROVISED WEAPONS

You don't have to spend a lot of money to have an effective weapon for self-protection. In fact, there are a handful of items you may already have around the house or can pick up at the local hardware store for just a few dollars. The set of steak knives in your kitchen notwithstanding, here are a few of my favorites:

Wasp Spray

Wasp spray—manufactured to take out wasp's nests—makes

a great weapon for slowing or stopping an attacker from a safe distance. The canister emits a condensed line of heavy foam that can travel straight as an arrow for 20 – 25 feet with amazing accuracy! To me, this is a better option than the aerosol sprays, like mace or pepper spray, at least for home defense or at the office, just because of the extra space it allows between you and the attacker. Be sure to purchase a brand that has a finger slot trigger, which makes it impossible to shoot the spray at yourself even if you're in the dark. If you can get the foam near an assailant's eyes, it will be effective in temporarily blinding him, giving you time to escape or to follow up with a few shots from your hardwood baton.

Awl

An awl resembles a screwdriver, except its metal shaft ends in a point. It costs about $8 and is made for puncturing wood, but it can just as easily puncture skin, making it a lethal weapon (one that is completely legal to purchase and carry, or keep in the glove box of your car). Similarly, a stitching awl looks more like an ice pick and is used for puncturing holes in leather. It's equally as effective at puncturing arteries and vital organs, maybe even more so if your assailant is wearing a leather jacket! Of course, a Phillips-head screwdriver also makes for a good contrived weapon for puncturing, and a heavy-duty socket wrench is excellent for delivering blunt force trauma. But the practical uses of these tools make it easy for you to use them for a repair job and then forget to put them back in your nightstand! By contrast, how many times will you use an awl around the house or car? Exactly! That's why an awl will stay where you put it and be there when needed.

Heavy-Duty Flashlight

A heavy-duty "D" battery-sized flashlight (such as a Maglite) makes for a great makeshift baton, and many specialized tactical flashlights feature a serrated bezel that can be used as an improvised striking device during an attack. Since you should have a working flashlight next to your bed and in your car anyhow, why not have one that can be used to break an intruder's collarbone as well?

FOUND IMPROVISED WEAPONS

A lot of ordinary things can be used as immediately improvised weapons. Even a tightly rolled up magazine can be dangerous if jabbed into someone's face or throat. The main point is, before you're under attack, take a moment to survey your daily surroundings for anything that may give you an advantage. Do it at your home, office, car, and classroom. Think: will it puncture? Will it cause blunt force trauma? Will it burn, blind, or stun? Here is a partial list of everyday items, which can often be found in and around the home or office and are immediate improvised weapons if needed:

- Fire extinguishers (to temporarily blind and cause respiratory issues from the chemicals, and to cause blunt force trauma if used as a heavy object to strike)
- Pot of hot coffee to the face
- Coffee or beer mug to the ear area
- Aluminum water bottle to the ear area
- Keys to the face (sharp ends held individually between fingers in a fist)
- Belt buckle to the face
- Golf clubs to the body or ear area
- Ball point pen to the eyes or throat
- Scissors to the throat or abdomen
- Umbrellas and canes to the wrists, lower legs, or ear area
- Desk lamp to the ear area
- Box cutter to the throat
- Tire iron to the ear area or lower legs
- Pliers to the eyes or throat
- Corkscrew to the eyes or throat
- Cooking pans or rolling pins to the ear area
- Water glass or soda can (held from the bottom) smashed into the face

The key to improvised weapons is to use them without hesitation. Don't pick up any weapon (newly found or pre-arranged) for the purposes of threatening someone; they may easily end up taking it and using it against you, and you've eliminated the critical advantage of surprise. If you picked up an improvised weapon to begin with, it's because you feel threatened. Using it first—before the assailant can process what's happening and react—is how you gain the upper hand.

9

COMING TO THE AID OF OTHERS

Remember the story from earlier in the book, when I was eleven, sitting towards the back of a bus, traveling home from a day at the beach? A handful of gang members boarded and began assaulting and otherwise harassing the driver and other passengers. As they menaced their way down the aisle, their 20-year-old leader spied and honed-in on me. He stopped within a foot or two of where I was sitting, shouted something, and then lunged towards me.

In the chapter on *The Law of Self-Defense*, I hope that I sufficiently articulated the law and provided a persuasive argument to support the conclusion that I could have justifiably used force to defend myself—even to strike first—at that time, but that's not what happened. For starters, I was only eleven, and I was frozen with fear, as one might expect at that age especially.

Here is what occurred that day. Like I said, I was frozen in my seat, terrified, as the gang leader sprung forward to grab me. Suddenly, the guy sitting behind me—a man in his early sixties I would guess, who looked like all the world to be an ex-con—stood and without hesitation threw a wicked punch across my seat, striking the gang leader squarely in the face. The force of the blow knocked the gang leader to the floor. Within seconds, the older guy was hovering over the fallen gang leader, where he proceeded to punch him another couple of times.

The bus came to a screeching halt. The area around where I was sitting was splattered with blood. The gang leader staggered to his feet. He looked from his blood-stained clothes to the guy who hit him. Maybe it was a result of the unexpected, violent, and direct action, the older guy's physical appearance, or a combination of the two, but I saw fear register on the leader's face. The gang members (who too had remained frozen because of the suddenness of the older guy's actions) now rushed to their leader's aid. They grabbed him and dragged him from the bus. The older gentleman stayed on the bus, screaming at the fleeing, former tough guys. Now that I think back on it, a thank you note to my guardian angel that day would have been appropriate!

I had just witnessed the "use of force for the protection of others," another occasion where the law recognizes that circumstances exist which justify an action, providing a defense for what would otherwise be a charge of battery or worse. Basically, this rule says that someone is justified to use force to protect a third person if that third person would have been justified in using that same force under those circumstances. To borrow from an old Broadway song, it's not "Anything you can do, I can do better," but "Anything you can do, I can do the same." Akin to the law of self-defense, the person defending another must reasonably believe that an attack on the other person is imminent (or is occurring) and intervenes using reasonable force. Stated differently, the person defending another is stepping into the proverbial shoes of the person they are defending.

So, it shouldn't be surprising that the law on the defense of others tracks the law of self-defense. This includes condoning the lawful use of deadly force if the person employing such force reasonably believes that a third person is in danger of imminent death or serious bodily injury. Keep in mind however, as a third party coming to the aid of another, any justification for self-defense goes out the window if the third party is the initial aggressor. And like the law of self-defense, the person coming to the defense of another can be wrong in assuming imminent danger and serious bodily harm was about to occur to another person, so long as they were reasonable as to their belief and actions taken. Moreover, the action taken doesn't have to be solely against the actual assailant, but can be directed instead against anyone assisting the assailant.

———

Now let's return to the fight I was involved in as a teenager at Trader Joe's. If you recall, I rushed over to my friend Brian, who was bloody, on the ground, and being kicked in the face by the guy who had been driving the other car. I slammed the guy kicking Brian into a brick wall at full speed, breaking his nose: all justifiable under the law of the defense of others.

Or was it?

Leading up to my action, words had been exchanged between Brian, myself, and the occupants of the other vehicle when both cars were in front of Trader Joe's. Generally, though, words alone will not provide justification for the use of force to defend oneself or another. When the cars stopped in the alley behind Trader Joe's, it had been Brian who was the first to jump out of either car. It was also Brian who ran to the other vehicle. Finally, it was Brian who proceeded to initiate the physicality by headbutting the driver through the driver's open window. Arguably, Brian was the aggressor. Arguably, I had no right to defend a third-party aggressor.

Okay, but there are other arguments that can be made here. For example, one argument could be that Brian had lost his "aggressor" status as he was being kicked into unconsciousness—so then I could legally defend him. Remember, an aggressor can gain the right to defend themselves if they've communicated that they're withdrawing from the fight but the other person continues with their assault. If you, in one way or another "tap out," the physical attack against you legally must stop. Well, I'd argue that an individual bordering on unconsciousness clearly has withdrawn his intention of fighting any longer and has withdrawn. When you're incapacitated, you're tapped out, and I would argue that I could now legally come to his aid and defend him.

Another argument could be that I had acted in self-defense rather than in the defense of another. I had already subdued a skinhead who had come after me unprovoked, and I had another guy pointing a gun at me at the time of my action. I feared something imminent was going to happen to me if I didn't do something. But in claiming self-defense, shouldn't I have gone for the guy pointing the gun directly at me rather than the guy kicking Brian? Arguably, the guy pointing the gun at me should have put me in reasonable fear of imminent bodily harm, not the guy with his back to me kicking someone else. I'd make a complicity or aiding and abetting argument—the kicker was an accomplice to the guy assaulting me with the gun, and under the legal theory of accomplice liability, the accomplice, basically, stands in the same shoes as the assailant. I'd argue, on this point, that I could go after the accomplice in the same way I could have gone after the actual assailant.

Brian and I were lucky that no charges were filed against us, and since I never had to make any legal defense in my case, I say, enough of this intellectual exercise. But I did want to relay the law and show you that the way that the facts unfold in a particular situation do matter when it comes to interpreting the law. Moreover, my episode is an example of how you, yourself, can potentially end up being the one who is arrested and charged with assault and battery, even in a situation that starts innocently enough (assisting an old lady) but escalates into violence with others.

Regardless of the legality of defending myself, or my friend, what about some sort of duty to intervene, be it a friend or a stranger? Not surprising, generally, there is none under the law. The law does not require you to intervene and come to the aid of another, even if you're shielded by the law for the actions you take, assuming they are reasonable. So, if the law doesn't require action, but protects reasonable action, shouldn't there be some thought as to what each of us as individuals should do?

Who knows what would've happened to me if a stranger hadn't reached across the bus seat and punched the gang leader in the face. What drove this stranger to intervene? He had no obligation. I believe most of us know in our hearts and minds what we should do in situations when we see others in imminent danger. We should do what the stranger on the bus did for me, especially since I was defenseless kid. Regardless of age, size, or strength, however, there are vulnerable people all around us, and they may be as defenseless as an 11-year-old because they are too gripped by fear to fight back. You will recognize it now, and there should be no question, no hesitation. Others might look away from someone in need for no other reason than the fear of being late to work or school. Others will look away out of fear of being injured, getting their new shirt soiled, or being called into the police station as a witness to a crime. And there's always the fear of being named in a meritless lawsuit for your actions, further underscoring the maxim that "no good deed goes unpunished." These fears are easy to switch off because they aren't legitimate fears, just excuses.

But what if it was *your* daughter, son, mother, brother, or spouse under attack? Wouldn't you hope that humanity and compassion would prevail and motivate someone, anyone, to come to their aid? Of course you would, and humanity includes you! Yes, there are inherent risks when inserting yourself into a volatile encounter, and good Samaritans are sometimes killed while doing courageous acts. And let me be clear, I'm not campaigning for suicide missions. If you can assess that coming to the aid of another person carries a high risk of being killed yourself, don't be a martyr. Focus instead on getting you and others around you to safety, and call the police. If the threat against another person is serious but appears less lethal than say, a visibly armed aggressor poised to fire a gun or stab with a knife, then act quickly before his empty hands are replaced with a weapon.

You know what to do now because you've read about and seen demonstrative photos and videos demonstrating the techniques on how to neutralize an assailant. These techniques (especially the proactive use of fast hand combinations) are just as effective for your own self-defense as they are for coming to the aid of others. Because you have these tools and the confidence to act to protect yourself, use these same tools and confidence to aid someone who needs defending. It's the right thing to do, what you hope others would do for you or someone you love, and it very well may be saving their life.

10

INTIMATE PARTNER VIOLENCE

Intimate partner violence, also commonly called "domestic violence," didn't fit into the section on *Awareness of Environment* because while it most often starts in the home, the environment isn't the contributing factor. Instead, it's about the abuser and the victim. That said, it also doesn't quite fit into the section on *Awareness of Individuals*, as the abuser and the victim are no strangers to one another. Yet it cannot be ignored.

A woman is beaten every nine seconds in the U.S., and 1 in 4 women will be victims of severe violence by an intimate partner during their life. Sadly, about 1,500 people each year are murdered by an intimate partner (spouse, partner, boyfriend, or girlfriend); the majority are women, but not all, and they are often especially brutal, involving beatings, stabbings, and strangulation.

I'm not a mental health expert, so I don't want to provide advice where I'm not qualified. And even where I am quali-

fied (in providing individuals with information and instruction on their personal defense), intimate partner violence is
admittedly complicated to understand and requires giving
advice to victims who often are (in their own minds) absolutely certain the danger has passed. Nevertheless, I want to,
at a minimum, present what I've learned about the mindset
of the intimate partner abuser and of the abused, as well as
suggest some things we can do if we suspect or know of intimate partner violence, regardless of whether we are mental
health professionals.

Author and security consultant Gavin De Becker calls
domestic abuse deaths "America's most predictable
murders." He explains that the warning signs are all around
and are anything but subtle. A victim will simultaneously
have a strong sense of being at risk for even more violence
from her intimate partner, but hopeful that the most recent
incident of brutality will be the last. She sees her spouse
resolving conflicts with intimidation—threatened or actual
violence against her or the children—and then just as
quickly, he minimizes the episode. An abusive spouse may
throw and break things, often under the influence of alcohol
or drugs, and these substances are frequently used as an
excuse for his extreme behavior. There's no need for
someone to check off every box for them to qualify as a wife
beater, but chances are good that he's a guy who cannot
accept rejection, is paranoid, jealous, uses money for the
purposes of control, and keeps his victim on a tight leash. He
likely has a weapon or talks about guns or other weapons
frequently.[19]

Predictably, the escalation of domestic violence in a relationship typically involves more than just observations of character traits and recent behavior. There's usually a long-term pattern of violence often including the abuse of a former wife or girlfriend, the existence of an abusive parent in the husband's family while growing up, or police records of previous domestic violence incidents. What most of us can't wrap our heads around is why anyone would stay in an abusive relationship. If it's a matter of choice (and it is), then why not just leave?

The truth is, far too many women choose to stay, for reasons we may find difficult to understand, unless you, yourself, have been victimized by an abusive spouse, or you're a professional who has been educated on the complex subject of battered wife syndrome. I'm neither of these, but what I have learned has given me awareness, empathy, and the realization that intimate partner violence is a unique type of situational violence, one that doesn't neatly fit into my self-defense system. How can I help someone stay safe when they have already stopped defending themselves?

I was shocked to learn that battered women get a strong sense of relief when the beating incident is over, so much so, that the relief they experience becomes addictive. The abuser is in control and does everything to maintain his power over the victim. He decides if today will be one of calm or of mayhem, and flips between delivering sweet words and gestures, and bruises and black eyes. He verbally paints romantic vistas of the way things used to be and swears it will never happen again. Unfortunately, it works. The battered spouse clings onto the powerfully pleasant feelings of the guy she once knew and in many ways still loves.

Worse, she has been too traumatized to objectively challenge the elephant in the room, clinging onto the hope that yesterday's beating will surely be the last.

Meanwhile, the cumulative psychological damage to the victim is nearly as bad as the physical violence suffered. After being trained over months or years not to resist the beatings, the abused victim loses their instinct to protect themselves (the fight or flight response is short-circuited), leaving them to wrestle with the opposing and equally powerful instinct to stay close to family, because family feels safe.[19]

How can my system of self-protection offer any value when the victim chooses to stay in an environment that shows the strongest signals of additional, imminent violence, and to stay with "friends" that engage regularly in dangerous, high-risk behaviors—the same two red flags of potential victimization that I warned about earlier in this book? As you also read earlier, every self-protection style—and every system—has its weaknesses, including my own, Kuaishou, which at its core requires an absolute commitment to deliver controlled violence on an attacker without hesitation, proactively, and with speed and fury. Without this mindset—the commitment to defend your life with every fiber of your being—no system, not even mine, can help you protect yourself or your children. This is why I'm suggesting a different self-protection tactic for those women who take the courageous but essential step to leave their intimate partners. Let me explain.

Set aside for the moment the notion that killing a wife or girlfriend is a so-called "crime of passion." The reality is that the murder of a family member is almost always a decision requiring preparation, not a spontaneous overreaction to an emotionally charged argument. Murders rarely occur in the "heat of battle," and most happen when the couple is no longer living together. In fact, 75% of domestic partner murders happen after the spouse leaves the relationship.

Wait! I thought leaving the relationship was the safest choice?

It's the right thing to do, but it requires some planning and a defensive strategy. Why? It goes back to one of the predictors of domestic abuse: the man who can't handle rejection. Your decision to leave the relationship is obviously rejection to the spouse, and it's going to be known soon by friends and family. It's a humiliating blow to the abuser. If the angry husband or boyfriend becomes a stalker, or begins otherwise harassing and threatening, one frequently recommended course of action is to file a police report and obtain a court-ordered temporary restraining order, or TRO. If you're a victim, or a friend of a victim, and this is the advice you are given, I urge you to think twice and do your own research. A 2018 *Washington Post* investigation of domestic killings in five major US cities revealed that 36% of the men who murdered had a previous restraining order against them. It appears that issuing a restraining order is often perceived as an act of war by the recipient, who may respond weeks or months later viciously and violently.[20]

———

If you know someone who is a victim of domestic violence, what should you do?

Speak up! The worst thing you can do is stay silent. Whether you're a family member, friend, neighbor, coworker, teacher, or doctor, if there is suspicion of violence, report it to the police. Guide the victim or the abuser to seek professional help. Abused women should be referred to a battered women's shelter. They can speak with people who understand what the victim is going through. Abusive men can also contact battered women's shelters for referrals to treatment programs.

If You Are the Victim

Reach out to a battered women's shelter or call a regional domestic abuse hotline for guidance and support. Many shelters are kept in secret locations for your protection. You can search the Internet for a walk-in shelter near you that will accept you and your children today. Be sure to clear your search history from the browser on the device you use, and leave no clues behind for your abusive intimate partner. Another (and safer) option is the local public library. Not only does the library have free access to computers for searching information on the web, they have someone to assist you if needed. If you're hesitating about the advice you've just read, understand that the ultimatum you have outlined in your mind—but have not yet delivered to your intimate partner—is destined to fail. Offering him "one last chance" is just continuing that walk down a potentially deadly path. Gather the kids and get out now. Some jurisdictions will take custody of your children away from you for allowing the kids to witness the violence you've endured and failing to report it to the police.

A self-defense course for women who are threatened or stalked by a former spouse or boyfriend is helpful but it may not be enough. It's one thing to teach the importance of awareness, and to train students to deal with a sudden threat or attack, but when the threat is known to you, stalking you, and motivated by revenge, they will use a weapon, likely on their own terms and at their day and time of choosing. This is one of the very few instances where I recommend not only a self-protection course, but that you also consider the purchase of a firearm and enrolling in a gun safety and training course. A good self-defense course will help you develop the proper mindset required to pull the trigger, if necessary, and the weapon provides an effective, lethal means to stop someone who is determined to make you pay the price for your "rejection." Again, without the conviction to fight back, weapons and less lethal self-defense techniques are worthless. The proper mindset to engage and attack a threatening person assumes the person being attacked values their life and the lives of their children. Sadly, battered women are often made to feel worthless by their abusive partner. The care and support from a battered women's shelter can help restore self-worth and confidence.

PART III

WHEN TO ENGAGE

If you've been the target of a serious threat of bodily harm or a life-threatening violent encounter, you probably already know it's almost never as simple as choosing to run, hide, or fight. There are additional variables at play: the number of attackers, available light, escape routes, the screaming and panic of the people around you, the terror of the sound and smell of bullets being fired, glass shattering, or wounded people falling around you. Maybe your wife and kids are with you. The essential point I'm trying to make is that while every dangerous situation will be different and challenging, the faster you can process what's happening around you, the quicker your response calculus will be, allowing you to act faster and improve your chances of survival. Devoting a few moments ahead of time to think through what actions you would take in a potentially violent encounter will better prepare you to quickly calculate your best response. Of course, you can't rehearse for every possible violent encounter, but you can think through various responses that make the most sense in certain situations. The type of aggressor is a good place to start. Are you engaging with an idiot, a monster, or someone in between?

Dealing with idiots—rude, intoxicated, or belligerent people—are the more common threats you're likely to encounter in your lifetime, and they're also the easiest to avoid; simply ignore them and walk away. These people didn't wake up in the morning wanting to kill you, but stupid arguments can escalate to out of control in a matter of seconds and lead to serious injury, or worse. If you can't walk away from them (because you're on a moving train, or the aggressor follows you, or is blocking your only exit path), maintain a safe distance and keep the troublemaker out of your attack zone. Shout short, simple commands if necessary: "Stop! Stay Back!" If the aggressor fails to heed your instructions and enters your attack zone, you're now facing a clear and imminent threat—you must engage! No more warnings. Don't make any threats or ask questions about why he's doing what he's doing. Attack! Fight first and fight fast, with sufficient force to stop the troublemaker from continuing his threatening behavior, but no more.

On the other end of the threat continuum are people who (for whatever reason, or no reason) intend to kill you, or simply don't care if the outcome of the confrontation ends with you bleeding out on a lonely sidewalk around the corner from an all-night taco truck. These are the monsters. Statistically speaking, situations where you'll need to literally fight for your life are statistically low. It happens, of course, but the very idea of it happening *to you* is probably so remote and unexpected that it will freeze you in a moment of disbelief. Precious seconds are squandered through inaction while you try and wrap your brain around something you've never experienced or expected to experience.

You'll sharpen your personal defense mindset, eliminating hesitation, if you recognize and act instantly to a threat requiring you to unleash a proactive, violent attack on someone—before they make YOU the victim. Similarly, faster recognition of a threat which is neither imminent nor serious keeps you from acting unnecessarily or with excessive force.

Here are some examples of situations which would cause me to proactively engage a person the instant I recognized them as a potential threat:

1. Any hostile person who confronts me and enters my attack zone despite my warning for them to stay back. Or, any able-bodied person acting or sounding threatening who steps immediately into my attack zone.

2. Any instance of someone who breaks into my house or attempts entry into my car.

3. Any disgruntled former employee that returns to my workplace and argues about or ignores a specific request to leave the premises immediately.

4. When witnessing an innocent person being intimi-

dated, harassed, or assaulted, and where I can intervene intelligently (without becoming a martyr).

There are only four. That's right. There are only four situations that—if they occurred—I would act out of default,
without hesitation to attack, and attack first. These four
scenarios require a proactive self-protection response to
disrupt the bad guy's intentions before he turns physical
toward you or someone else.

Some situations, however, require reactionary responses,
but these too call for split-second decisions and deliberate
action to thwart a disaster. Reactionary responses become
necessary because, perhaps even despite your best efforts,
you find yourself in a situation where the criminal managed
to gain the upper hand. In these instances, you must wait for
that narrow opportunity to escape or fight back. It may be a
mere fraction of a second, but you must act when the opportunity first presents itself. If the criminal gets momentarily
distracted, turns his back to you to see if anyone is witnessing
the crime, or brandishes his weapon within striking distance
of your hands or feet, I would attack fast and furiously. Here
are three scenarios where I would accept the risks involved
with acting—despite the criminal's advantage of a weapon—
at the first possible moment of distraction, because what's
coming next may give the criminal an advantage too superior
to overcome:

1. Any attempt to move me to a secondary location.
(Forget about what you see on TV. Rarely does it ever
end well at a secondary crime scene).

2. Any attempt to restrain me with rope, zip ties, or duct tape.

3. Any active shooter where you can get to the weapon during the shooter's reloading (usually 5-7 seconds or more, depending on their experience with firearms), or where you are close enough to attack effectively from the shooter's blind spot.

Those are another three instances where my default response is burned into my memory, for a total of seven default responses; four proactive and three reactive. There's no need to memorize a long list of situations where you must engage. It's not complicated. In virtually every other threatening situation, your best options are to run or hide.

If Robbed at Gunpoint

If you're confronted by someone who shows a gun or knife and demands your wallet, purse, keys, or watch, consider this: if that person really wanted to kill you, you'd be dead already. Why tempt fate? All your stuff is replaceable, but you are not. Give the gunman your wallet or whatever material object he demands, but deliberately toss it to the ground in the opposite direction you intend to run, and then run! Criminals don't chase their victims, unless perhaps you're a target for kidnapping, and there's no reason for them to try and shoot you in the back when they already have what they want. If you've had training, it's not difficult to disarm someone if they happen to be pointing the gun or knife at you from inches away. Seriously though, other than the movies, that almost never happens. More likely, the gunman will maintain a safe distance of several feet. An expert could still disarm the criminal at this distance, but probably not you. At six feet away or more, even an expert will tell you that you're better off tossing the wallet and running than trying to disarm the criminal.

As I wrote earlier, giving some thought to your default responses to threatening people and situations sharpens your personal defense mindset and speeds reaction time, those precious seconds that can make the difference between becoming a survivor or a victim of brutality. The following chapter provides six different and potentially violent situations. Call it a dress rehearsal for avoiding or surviving violence—a performance I sincerely hope you'll never see, but if you do, it won't be the first time you've given some thought to: what you would do?

11

RESPONSE CALCULUS: ASKING YOURSELF – WHAT WOULD YOU DO?

Remember those exotic and sometimes poisonous spiders my father had as "pets?" He brought most of them back from a trip to Hawaii. He and I searched for them in the rainforests of Waimea (he was in front), and my dad would collect them in Tupperware containers that he held on his lap for five hours in his first-class airline seat during the return flight home. He let them roam freely in our basement, which I think was technically a bomb shelter built by the original owner of our house on Roses Road.

My brother Robbie and I also used this space under the house for weightlifting. It was cooler down there than outside in the yard, and it kept the equipment dry. My father loved his eight-legged creatures; he fed them regularly, and they grew bigger and bigger, but they never bothered us and we didn't bother them. One afternoon, Mark Mathias, my brother Robbie's friend, called my dad's office to ask if it was okay if he worked out in our basement. My dad agreed, but warned him to stay clear of the large and poisonous spiders that had by now spun enormous webs in the corners of the cellar. Undeterred, Mark made his way to our house, pumped iron for an hour or so, then stopped inside the house to chat. My dad was home by now and reading in his study. Mark poked his head through the door and thanked him for the use of the weight room. "Oh, and by the way Dr. Kerr," he added proudly, "I took care of that spider problem you had down there!"

Misunderstandings can be deadly. Mark was simply being proactive to a perceived threat, even though the spiders showed no interest in him, made no threatening moves, or shouted insults at him about his mother. He wiped out my father's prized collection of spiders based solely on the stereotype that spiders—especially poisonous spiders—were a nuisance and evil, and should be killed. Had my father educated Mark about the true nature of the creepy cellar dwellers, they would have lived long and happy spider lives. The situation would have ended with a far better outcome for my father too. All of this is just a reminder that just because someone or something doesn't look like you, doesn't mean they deserve to be smacked with a broomstick. Multiple anomalies in a given situation is a more reliable indicator of danger, never appearances alone.

At this point, you've read about the value of awareness, of environments that lend themselves to specific dangers, and about individual awareness, from idiots to criminals and antisocial monsters. And you've read about awareness of self, and in so doing, taking a moment to stop pointing your finger in blame at everyone else and instead turning it back toward yourself to assess if you (and your ego) have contributed to the problems of bullying or violence against others. You've read about the laws of self-defense, and about many of my own encounters with violence, much of it self-inflicted during my youth. And you've read other accounts in this book of people who have been victims of bullying, abuse, or violence, which, perhaps with some previous knowledge and training, may have avoided the situation altogether, or at least met the threat with decisive action. Lastly, you've read about paying attention to that gut feeling inside you—your intuition—that loyal, single-minded superpower you already possess that will steer you clear of many potentially dangerous situations, if you listen to it.

I'd now like to provide you with some real-life violent encounters and ask you to ponder—with all your previous experience, as well as your newfound knowledge—how you would respond had you encountered these situations. After reading the summary of each true event, look away from the book for a moment and ask yourself: what would you do?

THE BELLIGERENT TRAIN PASSENGER

Situation: An intoxicated and belligerent passenger is screaming racist remarks and threatening a pair of frightened teenage girls near you on the same commuter train.

What would you do?

On May 26, 2017, students and workers alike packed into the late afternoon light-rail commuter trains in Portland,

Oregon as they headed home for what promised to be an exceptionally hot and sunny Memorial Day weekend. On one train, passenger Jeremy Joseph Christian—later identified as a 35-year-old self-described white supremacist—began shouting racially charged hate speech and threats at two teenage Muslim girls onboard as he drank sangria from a brown paper bag. Among other things, Christian, disheveled and wide eyed, ridiculously accused the girls of being involved with the terrorist group ISIS and screamed at them, "Go home. We need Americans here," and "Get off the train, you don't pay taxes." It was impossible for others nearby not to overhear the verbal abuse, including three fellow passengers: Micah Fletcher, Taliesin Namkai-Meche, and Rick Best, who intervened on the girls' behalf.

Jeremy Christian, the aggressor, stood up and shoved Fletcher in the chest, and Fletcher similarly shoved him back. Christian then pulled a folding knife from his pocket, concealing it in his hand. Christian dared Fletcher to hit him again, and then stabbed Fletcher in the neck. He then proceeded to stab a second passenger, Namkai-Meche, in the neck. Rick Best, a third passenger, who got up to help the victims under attack, was himself stabbed in the neck by Christian. At that moment, the train had just arrived at Portland's Hollywood Transit Center. Christian again stabbed two of the victims again before leaving the train. He proceeded to scream at and threaten passengers on the platform before wandering out of the station. Police arrested Christian several blocks away. Taliesin Namkai-Meche and Rick Best died from their stab wounds. Fletcher survived but was critically wounded.

Here, three individuals came to the aid of two teen girls being terrorized by an intoxicated and racist fellow passenger who was demanding the girls get off the train, and sadly, their efforts met with tragic results. So, in hindsight, should they have gotten involved in the first place?

It's easy to sit in judgment and speculate using hindsight, but this has nothing to do with ego. This has everything to do with having the proper training inside and out to try and prevent it from happening again. We owe that to these three men and their families.

Let's review the facts:

A passenger drinking sangria from a brown paper bag while riding the local Metro train isn't by itself an immediate cause for alarm. As you read earlier, there are usually several indicators that when combined, signal possible, imminent trouble. Christian's disheveled appearance only added to an overall impression of someone who wasn't concerned about grooming or hygiene; his appearance was an outward message that he could care less about fitting in and probably didn't have real friends. Add the loud and hostile demands shouted at the two young girls on a crowded train, and this was now anything but normal for the environment or situation.

Belligerent. Threatening. Intoxicated. There's no reasoning with a person in that state, and aboard a moving train, there's no escape. There was only one course of action to take if action was to be taken at all. Christian should have been told in short, clear words to shut up and stay in his seat. In the very fraction of a second he failed to comply, the best course of action would be to strike him swiftly, violently, and unexpectedly to put him down and then keeping him down until the authorities arrived at the station. Anything less and, well, we see the carnage that can be caused by a deranged individual.

How could this tragedy possibly have ended with a better outcome? If your decision was to act (it would have been mine), I'll stress that in taking such action, it needs to be proactive, quick, and decisive, especially with a guy like Christian. Secondly, the cardinal rule: always assume that an individual has a weapon, if not multiple weapons, on them. Even without the knife, Christian had his sangria bottle, which he could've used as an improvised weapon. Had any of the passengers near the violent encounter been taught to always expect an unseen weapon, others could have been alerted to the possibility, or someone could have initiated a direct attack on the knife when seeing Christian's hand disappear into his pocket and quickly return.

THE FENDER BENDER

As you slow for a pair of dogs who run into the street, the car behind you bangs into your rear bumper. Both of you pull over and exit your respective vehicles. The other driver quickly approaches you. He's big, angry, and his neck is covered with tattoos. He immediately starts shouting and accusing you of recklessly hitting the brakes, resulting in the rear-end collision.

What would you do?

This incident above happened in San Bernardino, CA on New Year's Eve, 2017. Larry Falce, age 70, was a 36-year veteran with the San Bernardino County Sheriff's Department. At the time of the accident, in which Deputy Sheriff Falce was rear-ended as he attempted to break to avoid striking the dogs, he was off-duty and not in uniform. The driver of the car that struck Falce was Alonzo Leron Smith, a 30-year-old local gang member with a long criminal history. Both men exited their vehicles and an argument ensued. In less than two minutes, Smith threw a single punch to the side of the officer's head; Falce collapsed instantly and died, presumably when his head slammed against the pavement. The whole incident was captured on video by a local surveillance camera. Falce, a veteran and professional law enforcement officer, let his guard down for just a moment and tragically, it cost him his life.

This is an instance where you get back into your car and get out of there. It is obvious that anyone accusing someone else of needlessly braking is probably not going to be rational. And what if the other driver is covered in gang tattoos? This should be even more reason to not engage. Regardless, you don't want to argue with anyone who was just involved in a collision with you. They're already angry and upset, and looking to place blame on someone else. If you spot a hot head getting out of the other car, get back in your car, call 911 for help, and drive away if necessary.

TROUBLE WALKS INTO THE BAR

You're having a drink at a local pub, and in walk some unfamiliar guys who look like trouble: shaved heads, lots of ink around the skull and neck, and glazed eyes.

What would you do?

In December of 2017, at Gem City Grill—an old, established bar famous for its two-dollar beers, pool tables, and live music (and two blocks from where I live in Old Town Monrovia, California)—an incident occurred. A few guys with shaved heads, who were covered in gang tattoos, entered the bar, started arguing with a patron, and pulled out guns. One man died, two were wounded.

If you're in a bar and you see individuals who have the appearance of gang members, leave immediately, regardless of how cheap the beer is or how good the band may be. Here, all of the awareness we've been discussing should kick in—awareness of your environment and awareness of individuals—as well as your intuition. Even if you don't know what gang members look like, I think you have a good sense of what potentially dangerous people look like. So, you're now in a situation where anything can happen, especially with gang members who have no regard for life. Don't let the "anything can happen" happen with you in there.

LONE GUNMAN OPENS FIRE IN CLUB

You're in a loud, dark, and packed nightclub when a gunman enters and begins shooting with a semi-automatic rifle and a semi-automatic handgun.

What would you do?

This describes what happened at the Pulse Nightclub in Orlando, Florida on the night of June 12, 2016. The gunman murdered 49 young men and women and wounded 58 others. While these types of events are nearly impossible to prevent altogether, they are thankfully rare. Nevertheless, I can't help but think how things in Orlando could have ended differently. The club reportedly wasn't using metal detectors, checking bags, or patting down patrons that night, and although an off-duty policeman exchanged gunfire with the lone gunman early in the siege, many of the club-goers' instincts to hide during the 15-minute assault failed them that night.

Fourteen patrons of the club huddled together in a single handicapped bathroom stall during the assault, some of them praying, some texting final words of love to their families. Most of them were slaughtered when the terrorist eventually discovered them.

I don't blame any one of the club-goers for being gripped with panic and fear, for hiding in a restroom, or huddling together. It's what most people would instinctively do in a similar situation. And that's the problem. It may have taken only one person in that restroom with a small amount of knowledge or training to take a leadership role during the frightening situation and save most, if not all of the people trapped in the restroom, from dying.

Think about it: one gunman vs. fourteen adults. Yes, the gunman has a very powerful semi-automatic rifle and an automatic pistol, but there is no way he can kill everyone in that small room if you organize quickly and have the mindset to fight back. Station a couple of people behind the door, two others to the opening side, one high, one is low. Grab any improvised weapon available: a heavy trash can, a metal towel dispenser ripped from the wall, or even a piece of mirror glass smashed and chipped from the wall. When the gunman steps into the restroom (perhaps firing rounds) one person tackles his legs, another goes for the weapon. Those behind the door can push the door into the attacker to effectively limit his space to maneuver. Tackle and restrain the gunman immediately and always assume he has another weapon on him. If he's heavily armored (helmet, Kevlar vest) disable him with repeated strikes to his neck, or apply a chokehold until he loses consciousness. He may regain consciousness minutes after blacking out, so don't leave the attacker unrestrained until help arrives.

In most scenarios, again, the best thing to do with an active shooter is to determine quickly which direction the gunfire is coming from (remember: acoustics can play tricks), and then run in the opposite direction as far and as fast as you can out of the building. That's why, as discussed under awareness of environments, it's so crucial to take note of all exits in a venue when you first arrive. When panic ensues, certain exits may be in the line of fire or blocked from a stampede of people falling and stomping over each other to escape. If escape is not an option, be prepared to pick up a fire extinguisher, a paring knife, or a bottle of champagne and attack the shooter. The worst thing you can do is freeze and do nothing, which unfortunately again, is what most people do in these situations. Hiding behind a desk or dinner table also isn't recommended. Remember, a semi-automatic rifle round can penetrate a concrete wall. Chances are, there's no safety in hiding behind anything in a club short of a steel column, and in hiding, you'll need to hope (and pray) that the shooter doesn't open fire at the tipped-over dining table you're using as a shield.

How about changing the scenario just a little?

GUNFIRE AT AN OUTDOOR CONCERT

You and 15,000 others are enjoying a concert under the stars when suddenly gunshots ring out. So, you aren't necessarily confined by the interior of a building, yet there may not be many places to take cover.

What would you do?

This is what happened in Las Vegas on October 1, 2017, when a gunman opened fire from the 32nd floor of the Mandalay Bay Hotel, killing 58 people and wounding 800 during a performance by Jason Aldean on the third and final night of the Route 91 Harvest Music Festival. The scenario differs from The Pulse Nightclub in many respects and is closer to the tragic events experienced at the University of Texas at Austin on August 1, 1966. On that day, a sniper atop the Main Building tower randomly opened fire at students on campus and people on nearby streets, killing 16 and injuring 31.

In this tragedy, though people weren't limited in their escape options by the interior walls of a building, the perimeter fencing around the festival proved to be even worse. The fencing didn't adequately allow for the quick exit of thousands of people in an emergency, and there were no solid walls for concealment either.

Even once the people at the Harvest Music Festival realized they were hearing gunfire—instead of firecrackers—a good number of them unfortunately froze or laid on the ground for protection. Dozens of concertgoers were picked off systematically by the sniper, whose high perch delivered the gunfire from well above the victims on the ground. In this instance, ducking or lying down provided virtually no effective cover. People would again start running each time the gunman would stop firing to reload, only to then dive to the ground as the gunfire commenced. As I've pointed out in this book, don't lay on the ground when you have an active shooter...run! Run as quickly as possible in the direction opposite the gunfire to your pre-determined exit. Certainly, duck and cover if you need to evaluate the situation—which should only take seconds—but unless you're crouched behind two feet of concrete, your better chance of survival is going to be to run. Moving targets are harder to hit, especially from a distance, and running puts your fate into your own hands.

Also, unfortunately in these times, if you think you're hearing fireworks, you should quickly consider whether they're gunshots...gunfire can now happen virtually anywhere. Who would have expected gunshots at a Jason Aldean concert? But they were, and quicker recognition may end up saving your life.

COWORKER SHOWS SIGNS OF ABUSE

You suspect that the husband of a fellow employee may have beaten her. She denies it, but the bruises, her demeanor, and her lame excuses for the injuries to her face and body tell another story.

What would you do?

This is not a scenario where, assuming the spouse does not come to the place of employment, you are in danger per se, but rather consider this example as one where you're coming to the aid of another. Make it your business to help the person research a local battered women's shelter and offer to take her (and her children) to the safe location. There's a good chance she won't immediately accept your offer. Let her know this place will provide far greater safety than returning home, that they need to get help, and that they need to talk to someone. Help them to find the clarity and strength to make the decision to help themselves, and often their children as well.

Unfortunately, I lived this scenario twenty years ago, and I wish I knew then what I know now and had done things differently. A teacher, who taught in the classroom next to me and who had become a friend over the years, divulged to me that her husband, who suffered from mental illness, was becoming violent. As the violence continued and became more severe, she even began asking about training with me. And do you know what I did? Nothing. I felt that it was none of my business. This was something between a husband and a wife. And over the course of one weekend, her husband killed her. I should have intervened. I should have done something. To this day, I still live with this memory and the fact that I did nothing. I've learned a lot in twenty years so that you have no reason to carry the heavy weight in your heart that I have because of my failure to act.

12

THE PARTHIAN SHOT

The Romans greatly outnumbered the Parthians in the Battle of Carrhae. Crassus, their general, had already taken heavy casualties when the Parthians, an ancient Iranian people, feigned retreat, fleeing on horseback with the Romans in full pursuit. The Parthians had initiated their response calculus. As thousands of Parthians galloped into a canyon, Crassus was sure of an impending enemy massacre and a great Roman victory for himself. As the Roman infantry neared, suddenly the Parthian horse archers turned their upper bodies backward and began showering arrows upon them. The maneuver, known as The Parthian Shot, required incredible equestrian skills, with both of the rider's hands occupied with his bow. Stirrups had not yet been invented, and the soldier relied on pressure from his legs to guide his horse blindly. Unprepared and taken by surprise at the sudden fury of arrows, the Romans—now trapped by the canyon and under siege—were defeated by the much smaller

Parthian army. The Parthians were skilled, but also clever. The Romans were larger in numbers and experienced in battlefield tactics and fighting. At the end of the day, clever won out.

In my junior year of high school, I went looking for my own Parthian shot. It didn't come from an arrow. It came from a needle. It was 1986, and by that time I knew what my father's unique medical practice involved. I knew why the Hollywood action heroes, martial arts superstars, and Olympic and professional athletes were frequently at my house. Anabolic steroids, it seemed, made you bigger, stronger, and faster, and without as much weightlifting and work...very clever. The biggest game of my high school football career at the time was coming up, the final game of the season against our rival, Alhambra High. It was my chance to showcase my talents on the field and bring glory to my team and school.

I approached my father and asked him to give me something to help me play better than I had ever played, something to give me that edge over the competition, just as his patients had asked of him. He complied. But instead of administering an injection, he handed me a single capsule and instructed me to ingest the medication exactly one hour before kickoff. I followed his instructions and suited up for the game.

That night, on offense, I ran for 215 yards rushing and three touchdowns. On defense, I snagged three interceptions, two that I returned for two more touchdowns. I had 19 tackles, 16 of them solo, and 4 quarterback sacks. I was on fire! The following day, a picture in the local sports page captured me battling to cross the goal line with an Alhambra High defender tearing at my jersey in a desperate attempt to stop me from scoring again. We beat Alhambra High convincingly and I felt invincible.

I thanked my father for giving me the superpowers of the pill. I was sold and eager for more. Then, my dad, Dr. Kerr, opened the kitchen cabinet and pulled out a box of sugar and handed it to me. "This is what was in the capsule," he replied, and then walked away. My superpowers, as it turns out, came from a sugar pill, a placebo...or to be precise, from my own mind.

The modern-day phrase derived from the Parthian Shot is "parting shot," you know, those final words uttered as one leaves the room—usually a jab, or sometimes a cutting-edge quip. It's akin to dropping the microphone on the floor after having the definitive, last word. Dr. Kerr's placebo was his parting shot to me and perhaps to the 4,000 patients to whom he prescribed anabolic steroids. It was already in me to make the tackles, score the touchdowns, and break records like I did that night against Alhambra High, and my father knew it. I had worked and practiced hard for years, but questioned my confidence, letting fear seep into my thoughts before the biggest game of my high school football career.

In the more serious pursuit of reducing your chances of violent victimization, you too possess everything you need. Switch off the psychological and irrational fears that offer no value, and instead, trust your intuition, your gut feelings, that little voice in your head if it's telling you "I have a bad feeling about this guy" to alert you to potential threats. Despite your best efforts, if trouble finds you anyhow, gaining confidence to thwart a violent encounter improves with training. It doesn't require years of lessons and thousands of dollars to add basic attack and defense skills to your self-protection toolbox, but it does require you to make that commitment to research, select, and enroll in the proper martial art or self-protection course for you.

Meanwhile, we can all contribute to the cause of a world with less aggression and violence simply by relaxing, letting go of our stressors, and ignoring those people who seek to provoke needless fights. Whether it be through the practice of Qigong, or your own preference for methods of calming the mind and body, reducing stress and anxiety is crucial to self-control and a sense of overall well-being. Ultimately, when dealing with difficult or aggressive individuals, simple respect for others will defuse and deescalate almost all conflicts. Who we must not ignore, however, are victims of brutality, bullying, or intimate partner violence. I made that mistake once...never again.

We can also reduce violence by acknowledging our differences and putting a chokehold on the notion that everyone else must see the world like we do. Large spiders were harmless exotic pets to my father, yet to my brother's friend who saw the eight-legged creatures in our basement, they were threatening and needed to be killed. A little education from my dad to the over-exuberant executioner would have resulted in a better outcome.

Violence could ebb too if we question our stereotypes and prejudices, particularly how they influence our children. Sonny, my Muay Thai sensei and mentor, and the scariest person I had ever met at the time, was also a sought-after hairdresser to the stars. Ralph the Wolf didn't look as friendly as the other neighborhood dogs, but all he ever wanted was some affection (and your bologna sandwich). Looks alone aren't an indicator of a potential threat or criminal intent. We now know that physical attributes like anxious body language, or someone frequently patting their coat to make sure a weapon is still underneath. coupled with other behavioral anomalies, are more reliable.

On a final note, my father kept meticulous records of his famous patients. Even today you'd recognize many of the names, and almost none of them have admitted to using anabolic steroids to enhance their action movie careers or achieve Olympic glory. It doesn't seem fair that while other athletes fought to compete to the best of their natural abilities, others somehow had the ability to (metaphorically speaking) shoot arrows at them while riding backwards on a horse at full gallop. Maybe they had their incredible talents despite the anabolic steroids? Whatever the contribution these drugs may have had in the pursuit of Olympic medals, those athletes who used them didn't want anyone to know their secret, even after my father stopped prescribing them (due to widespread misuse) or when they were eventually banned from use in competition. Nor did a lot of the Hollywood stars. The death threats my father received (apparently to ensure that secrets remained secrets) he shrugged off, but for me they served as the catalyst of my self-defense passion and career. Unfortunately, those threats also made for some stressful and frightening times during my childhood, not just for me, but for my brothers and sister as well.

It's tempting to name names with my own parting shot,

but I'm going to ignore that opportunity. My only interest is in helping you and your family avoid violence or survive it. After a lifetime of hits to the head on the football field, bouncing drunks and idiots out of bars, skinhead monsters jumping out of Camaros, snakes, spiders, and strangers at my house, the last thing I'm looking to do is pick a fight.

ENDNOTES

1. The American Psychological Association. *The 2018 Stress in America Survey.* 2018, October 30.
2. Kerr, Robert, M.D. *The Practical Use of Anabolic Steroids with Athletes.* 1982.
3. Harris, Sam. Interview by Malcolm Gladwell [*Malcolm Gladwell's 12 Rules for Living,* podcast episode seven, season three].
4. Di, Wang (2016). The Impact of Mass Transit on Pulic Security. *Transportation Research Procedia, 25.* 3233-3252.
5. Danaher, Daniel Danaher.Tactical Encounters. Retrieved from http://www.*tacticalencounters.com*
6. Bars and Violence. PRC Resource Link. Retrieved from http://www.*Resources.prev.org/documents/saferbarsbackgroundes.doc*
7. Schrobsdorff, Susanna. (2016, October). Teen

Depression and Anxiety: Why the Kids Are Not Alright. *Time.*

8. Truman, J.L., Strand, M.R. (2010). *National Crime Victimization Survey, Criminal Victimization, 2009.* U.S. Department of Justice, Bureau of Justice Statistics. NCJ 231327.

9. National Safety Council. Is Your Workplace Prone to Violence. Retrieved from http://www.nsc.org/work-safety/safety-topics/workplace-violence. NSC, 2019

10. Becker, Galvin De. (1997). Chapter 9: Occupational Hazards. *The Gift of* Fear. Dell Publishing (Random House).

11. Szlemko, William. Benfield, Jacob. Bell, Paul. Deffenbacher, Jerry. Troup, Lucy. (2008). Territorial Markings as a Predictor of Driver Aggression and Road Rage. *J. Appl. Soc. Psychol.* 38,1664-1688.

12. Faris, Robert. Felmlee, Diane Felmlee. (2011). Status Struggles: Network Centrality and Gender Segregation in Same- and Cross-Gender Aggression. *American Sociological Review.*

13. Faris, Robert. Felmlee, Diane Felmlee. (2014). Casualties of Social Combat: School Networks of Peer Victimization and their Consequences. *American Sociological Review.* 79(2), 228-257.

14. Statista. (2017). *Americans with Tattoos Survey.* Retrieved from http://www.statista.com

15. Koch, Jerome. (2010). Body Art, Deviance, and American College Students.

16. Gibson, Chris Gibson. Fagan, Abigail. Antle, Kelsey. (2014). Avoiding Violent Victimization Among Youths in Urban Neighborhoods: The Importance of Street Efficacy. *American Journal of Public Health*.

17. Centers for Disease Control Prevention. The Relationship Between Bullying & Suicide: What We Know and What It Means for Schools. Retrieved from http://www.cdc.gov/violenceprevention/pdf/bullying-suicide-translation-final-a.pdf

18. Baxley, F. Miller, M. (2006) Parental misperceptions about children and firearms. *Archives of Pediatric and Adolescent Medicine.* 160(5), 542-7.

19. Becker, Galvin De. (1997). Chapter 10: Intimate Enemies. *The Gift of Fear.* Dell Publishing (Random House.)

20. Zezima, Katie. Paul, Deanna. Rich, Steven. Tate, Julie. Jenkins, Jennifer. (2018, December 9). Domestic slayings: Brutal and foreseeable. *The Washington Post*.

BIBLIOGRAPHY

Becker, Galvin De. (1999). *The Gift of Fear.* Dell Trade (Random House).

Gilliam, Jonathan Gilliam. (2017). *Sheep No More.* Post Hill Press.

Karidan, Steve Kardian. (2017). *The New Superpower for Women.* Simon & Shuster.

Koga, Robert. Pelkey, William, Pelkey, Ph.D., (2002). *Controlling Force: A Primer for Law Enforcement, 3rd Edition.* The Koga Institute.

Larkin, Tim. (2013). *Survive the Unthinkable.* Rodale Books.

Miller, Rory. (2008). *Meditations on Violence: A Comparison of*

Martial Arts Training & Real World Violence. YMAA Publication Canter.

Miller, Rory. (2016). *Training for Sudden Violence: 72 Practical Drills.* YMAA Publication Canter.

Horne, Patrick Van. Riley, Jason Riley. (2014). *Left of Bang.* Black Irish Entertainment.

INDEX

60 Minutes, 16

adrenaline, 6, 25, 101, 105, 114, 122, 190, 234

adrenaline-infused rage, 6

aggression, 10, 44, 49, 50, 63, 73, 100, 166, 300

alcohol, 30, 32, 35, 37, 44, 49, 63, 65, 80, 270

Alhambra High, 298

ambush, 18, 19, 34, 52

Anabolic steroids, 16, 298

anxiety
    reducing, 2, 100, 108, 300

Ariana Grande concert, 30

assault, 2, 4, 6, 12, 20, 23, 35, 40, 45, 48, 61, 65, 71, 75, 109, 128, 136, 139, 243, 261, 264, 280, 291

assaults
    random, 4

athletes, 7, 16, 17, 63, 190, 298, 301, 303, 313

attack zone, 25, 26, 27, 70, 83, 224, 278, 279
    calculating distance, 27

Attacking Forearm, 6, 187, 188, 189, 190, 233, 242, 245

attacks
    less lethal, 9

avoiding a violent
    encounter, 63, 66, 75, 95, 96

awareness, 7, 12, 13, 15, 17, 46, 55, 60, 76, 81, 85, 91, 125, 160, 269, 271, 275, 284, 290

awareness of environment, 284, 292

bars and clubs, 18, 36, 41, 49

baseline context, 18

batons, 21, 170, 248, 251

Bill Laich, 7

blocks, 4, 26, 150, 173, 223, 225, 226

body shots, 172, 174, 175, 190

breathing
    to reduce stress, 111

bullying, 45, 46, 48, 50, 66, 71, 72, 74, 134, 138, 140, 285, 300

Bureau of Justice, 12

burglars, 20, 248

Canadian investigators, 16

Canelo Alvarez, 225

centerline, 175

children present during a
    home invasion, 23

chokeholds, 159, 210, 219, 244, 292, 300

chokes, 171, 210, 214

Chuck Norris, 8

combat soldiers, 9

combination strikes, 240

coming to the aid of others, 261

commands used toward a
    threatening person, 25, 278

concealed weapons, 26

concerts, 30, 34, 79, 247, 293
    teens at, 34

confidence, 8, 10, 13, 47, 98, 101, 104, 122, 149, 156, 166, 267, 275, 299, 300

confined setting, 24

Controlling Adrenaline, 105

conviction, 101, 104, 122, 174, 275

counter attacks, 223

crime, 9, 12, 20, 24, 27, 45, 48, 65, 75, 81, 84, 91, 96, 101, 108, 249, 266, 272, 280

criminal activity, 18

criminal predators spotting
    easy targets, 41

criminals
    antisocial, 75

danger

respect for, 7
death threats, 7, 16, 301
Delivering Pain
  techniques, 169
dogs
  for protection, 21
domestic violence, 20, 269,
  270, 274
Drive Strike, 177, 178, 183, 184,
  186, 193
drug buyers and sellers, 20
drugs, 16, 24, 42, 48, 65, 97,
  240, 270, 301
ego, 6, 18, 39, 63, 66, 69, 70, 86,
  106, 107, 109, 117, 166, 287
engaging a threat
  when to, 277
escalated the situation, 5
escaping a rear choke, 219
ethnicity, 12
eye gouges and jabs, 207
FBI, 12, 21, 55, 77, 96
fear
  of strangers, 20
  overcoming, 101
  psychological, 110
fighting
  close quarters, 25, 161, 250
  for survival, 11, 104
fighting systems, 155
friends and activities
  impact of, 95
gang activity, 23
gangbangers, 8
GHB, 44
go time, 10
gunfire
  responding to, 33, 53, 293,
  294
Harvest Music Festival, 293
hate crimes, 12
head and neck strikes, 172,
191
head movement, 224
Hollywood, 17, 234, 286, 298
home invasions, 20
homicides, 21, 55, 128
hostile-aggressive
  individuals, 63, 64, 65, 66
inflicting pain, 171
Inside-Out Self-Protection,
  11, 83, 123
internal training, 6
intimate partner violence,
  269
intuition, 11, 13, 20, 28, 80, 83,
  86, 285, 290, 299
Jeet Kune Do, 8, 154
jiu-jitsu, 8, 79, 102, 156, 158,
  160, 165, 244
Jorge Linares, 174
Judo, 8, 79, 161, 165
karate, 8, 151, 156, 161, 164, 166
Ketamine, 44
kicks, 234
kids
  martial arts for, 164
knees, 239
Larry Falce, 289
Left of Bang, 18
Los Angeles, 16, 36, 249
LSD, 44
martial artists, 7
mass shootings, 30, 110
Mass transit stations
  crime, 24
MDMA, 43
Methamphetamine, 44
Metro bus, 26
Micah Fletcher, 286
mindfulness, 107, 110, 113, 117
mindset, 18, 29, 62, 76, 104,
  122, 161, 272, 275, 279, 282,
  292

Morley Safer, 16
Muay Thai, 8, 79, 153, 158, 161,
    300
multiple attackers, 243
murders, 21, 61, 68, 75, 77, 84,
    95, 108, 128, 130, 269, 270,
    272, 291
Okinawan karate, 7, 151
Olympic athletes, 17, 145, 201,
    298, 303
outside sphere
    of self-protection, 121
own worst enemy, 4
panhandlers, 20, 256
pepper sprays, 255, 256, 257
physical responses, 11, 81
predators, 27, 41, 91, 93, 101,
    104
profiling, 19
Qigong, 111, 112, 113, 114, 117,
    118, 119, 300
race, 12, 19, 65, 75, 81, 97
rape drugs. See club drugs
religion, 12, 65, 81
response calculus, 20, 277,
    283, 297
Rick Best, 286
road rage, 29, 67, 68, 69, 70,
    97, 109
robbed at gunpoint, 281
robbery, 12, 24
Robert Kerr, M.D., 7, 17
Rohypnol, 42
roofies. See Rohypnol
Route 91 Harvest Festival, 30
San Gabriel, 6, 8, 17, 77, 88,
    95, 96, 313
self-defense
    legal aspects, 125
self-protection
    experience, 103
self-protection instructors, 9

sexual orientation, 12, 75
Shotokan, 7, 8, 79, 151, 152
signs of abuse, 295
snakes, 7, 15, 21, 100, 302
spiders, 7, 21, 100, 224, 283,
    284, 300, 302
sporting events, 17, 30, 32, 39
sports associations, 16
Sports Illustrated, 16
sports medicine, 7
stress, 19, 46, 49, 63, 64, 81,
    103, 106, 107, , 108, 109, 111,
    113, 114, 117, 300
    APA Stress in America
        Survey, 2
strikes
    preemptive, 27
suicide bomber, 18
tailgate party, 30
Taliesin Namkai-Meche, 286
tattoos, 78, 80, 81, 87, 158, 288,
    289, 289, 290
techniques to deliver pain,
    169
terrorist attacks, 30
United States Marines, 18
University of Southern
    California, 8, 181, 313,
Vasiliy Lomachenko, 174
victimization, 30, 92, 96, 97,
    249, 272, 299
victims, 17, 39, 53, 54, 66, 68,
    70, 62, 73, 75, 76, 86, 138,
    139, 269, 270, 281, 285, 286,
    295, 301
violence
    at stadiums, 30, 31, 247
    controlled, 9, 272
    in the workplace, 55, 56,
        57, 59, 279
    on the road, 28
    self-inflicted, 4, 98, 109

senseless, 4
violent crimes, 9, 12, 48, 65,
    75, 82, 91, 97
weapons, 21, 26, 27, 34, 41, 46,
    51, 53, 54, 55, 69, 77, 82, 103,
    123, 131, 147, 161, 169, 170,
    179, 187, 213, 222, 228, 239,
    247, 248, 250, 253, 254, 256,
    258, 280, 288
well-being, 30, 106, 300
Wing Chun, 8, 25, 102, 147,
    148, 149, 150, 151, 154, 157,
    158, 166, 180, 184, 227

ABOUT THE AUTHORS

DAVID KERR, Master Instructor for Defense Kinetics, has more than three decades of experience in teaching mixed martial arts and boxing techniques specifically designed for self-protection. His students include professional athletes, law enforcement officers, business executives and professionals, as well as high school and college youths. Kerr grew up in San Gabriel, played football while attending the University of Southern California, and earned a Master's in History from Cal State University Los Angeles.

LUKE STROCKIS, CEO of Defense Kinetics, has trained under David Kerr for nearly a decade. He is an entrepreneur with more than 30 years of experience in starting and growing new businesses. He has worked in marketing, merchandising, and brand strategy for numerous worldwide brands including Mattel Toys, Disney Consumer Products, Warner Bros., Universal Studios, Nintendo, and Nike. He received his B.A. in Journalism from Cal State University Long Beach and a Masters from the Annenberg School at the University of Southern California.

HARRISON LEBOWITZ, writer, attorney, and entrepreneur, is a former New York City litigator and Assistant Attorney General with the state of Vermont. On the creative front, among other projects, Harrison coauthored a top ten national best seller, was a contributing writer for an Emmy award-winning series, wrote a NYC-produced musical, and has written optioned screenplays and scripts for TV/streaming. He received his B.A. in Chemistry from Franklin & Marshall College and his J.D. from The University of Baltimore School of Law.

DEFENSE KINETICS

INSTRUCTIONAL RESOURCES

- Idiots to Monsters Seminars
- Idiots to Monsters – The Podcast
- Personal Defense Instruction for Corporations
- Close Quarters Tactical Instruction for Law Enforcement
- Personal Defense Instruction for students and faculty of high schools, colleges and universities
- Personal Defense Training School, flagship facility, Pasadena, California
- Workplace Employee Defense Training and company-wide action plans

www.defensekinetics.com
info@defensekinetics.com
(888) 803-3566